Strategy Moves

FT Prentice Hall
FINANCIAL TIMES

In an increasingly competitive world, we believe it's quality of thinking that will give you the edge – an idea that opens new doors, a technique that solves a problem, or an insight that simply makes sense of it all. The more you know, the smarter and faster you can go.

That's why we work with the best minds in business and finance to bring cutting-edge thinking and best learning practice to a global market.

Under a range of leading imprints, including *Financial Times Prentice Hall*, we create world-class print publications and electronic products bringing our readers knowledge, skills and understanding, which can be applied whether studying or at work.

To find out more about Pearson Education publications, or tell us about the books you'd like to find, you can visit us at **www.pearsoned.co.uk**

Strategy Moves

14 complete attack and defense strategies
for competitive advantage

Jorge A. Vasconcellos e Sá

FT Prentice Hall

FINANCIAL TIMES

An imprint of Pearson Education

Harlow, England • London • New York • Boston • San Francisco • Toronto
Sydney • Tokyo • Singapore • Hong Kong • Seoul • Taipei • New Delhi
Cape Town • Madrid • Mexico City • Amsterdam • Munich • Paris • Milan

PEARSON EDUCATION LIMITED

Edinburgh Gate
Harlow CM20 2JE
Tel: +44 (0)1279 623623
Fax: +44 (0)1279 431059
Website: www.pearsoned.co.uk

First published in Great Britain in 2005

ISBN-10: 0-273-70167-3
ISBN-13: 978-0-273-70167-5

British Library Cataloguing-in-Publication Data
A catalogue record for this book is available from the British Library

Library of Congress Cataloging-in-Publication Data
A catalog record for this book is available from the Library of Congress

10 9 8 7 6 5 4 3 2
09 08 07 06

Designed by Sue Lamble
Typeset in 10/13.5pt Galliard with Frutiger by 70
Printed and bound in Great Britain by Henry Ling Limited, at the Dorset Press, Dorchester, DT1 1

The Publisher's policy is to use paper manufactured from sustainable forests

To my father and my uncle

Contents

Acknowledgements

This book tries to present new ideas as well as organizing existing ideas in a new framework, with many examples.

Among the authors I am indebted to, special credit should be given to Philip Kotler and Ravi Singh, who pioneered the field with their classic article 'Marketing Warfare in the 1980s', featured in the *Journal of Business Strategy* (Winter, 1981). Professor Kotler laid the foundations to support this book's further advancements.

It is hoped that the reader will benefit from both.

Preface: nothing is written

"The only thing certain about war is that nothing is certain about war."

Winston Churchill

"War is the stage of uncertainty."

Carl von Clausewitz

"In war, there is no guarantee of success. But we can make sure we deserve it."

Winston Churchill

IN HIS BOOK *Seven Pillars of Wisdom*, T. E. Lawrence – better known as Lawrence of Arabia – tells of an incident that happened as he was trying to seize Akaba from the Turks in World War I. Gasim, an Arab guerrilla warrior in Lawrence's army, fell asleep on his camel without anyone noticing. Thus he seemed to be condemned to certain death under the burning desert sun.

Miles away, when Lawrence noticed Gasim's absence he turned his camel around and journeyed into the desert alone, guided solely by an oil direction needle. It was an act of incredible audacity – almost madness.

'Don't go,' Prince Aura, one of the Arab leaders of the expedition, had advised him. 'You will never find him – and if by chance you do, he will certainly be dead. Even if he is not, you will never find your way back to us.' Lawrence insisted. Recognizing that he would not listen to reason, Aura declared fatalistically, 'It is useless. It is his destiny to die this way. It is written.'

Lawrence rescued Gasim and returned victoriously. When he finally joined the main army column, Lawrence smiled, 'Nothing is written – nothing,' he said.

This is one of the four major principles of this book: *nothing is written*. One can be small and win; equally, one can be large and lose. It all depends on how well one applies the rules of war. The leader who knows what strategies to carry out, when to perform them, and how to succeed in them, will win. The other leader loses.

Second, *these strategic rules are timeless*. Napoleon said, 'I fought forty battles and in the end I learned nothing I did not know before.' Success – both in business profitability and survival – depends on following the existing rules. Those who make the least errors seize the largest victories.

Third, because 'business is uncertain – just like war' (Carl von Clausewitz) – luck plays a significant part. To paraphrase Churchill, 'One can never be sure of success,' 'One can only deserve it.' Deserving it is only made possible by following the rules of strategy.

Finally, these rules are of utmost importance since in business there are no armistices – business is continuous and permanent. And in a war there are usually only two sides – in business there are many more. So business strategy, we argue, is more difficult than military strategy.

These four principles lead to a unique statement: *follow the rules*. Always. You may lose in the short term but you'll prevail in the long run. One may be defeated in battles but enjoy victory in the war. And you may run out of luck occasionally, but in the end you will overcome luck.

In Chapter 1 we show how one can lose with 5000 troops and win with a hundred. The military examples are taken from the British Zulu War in 1879, when the British suffered one of their greatest-ever defeats. At Isandlwana they lost more officers than at Waterloo and more men than at Inkerman or Alma. Then, on the same afternoon at the battle of Rorke's Drift, the British achieved an astonishing victory even though they were outnumbered by forty to one. Why? In Chapter 2 we examine why and explain the implications for business.

Chapters 5 to 7 present the 'what', the 'when', and the 'how' – which strategic movements should be carried out, how to co-ordinate them, and at what time.

Essentially there are 14 strategic movements. There are six types of *attack* – guerrilla; bypass; flanking; frontal attack; undifferentiated circle; and differentiated circle. These are outlined in Chapter 3. And there are eight types of *defense*: warning signals; creating entry barriers; global service; pre-emptive strike; block the entry; counter-attack; hold the ground; and withdrawal. These are shown in Chapter 4.

Chapter 5 demonstrates *when* to make one or another move, and Chapter 6 *how* to obtain help from strategic alliances.

Having laid out the conditions for success Chapter 7 then asks a specific question: how should firms internationalize? The answers are drawn from the experience of the Japanese car industry.

Finally, Chapter 8 summarizes the eight rules one must follow in order to deserve success. Since we cannot totally eliminate chance, how can we maximize the probability that the odds will be on our side and not against us? Chance is 'something that some complain about, while others make sure they earn it' (Lord Warell).

The structure of the book is summarized in Table A.1.

Table A.1 ◆ What, when and how

	Subject			
Chapter number	**What** (which strategic movements) and **how** (to do them)		**When**	**Other**
	Attack	**Defense**		
3	1 Guerrilla 2 Isolation 3 Flanking 4 Frontal attack 5 Undifferentiated circle 6 Differentiated circle			
4		1 Signaling 2 Creating entry barriers (fixed and mobile) 3 Global service 4 Pre-emptive strike 5 Counter-attack 6 Blocking the entry 7 Holding the ground 8 Withdrawing		
5			**When** to do each of the six attack and eight defense movements of Chapters 3 and 4	
6				The role of **strategic alliances**
7				Based on the **whats** and **hows** (of Chapters 3 and 4) and the **whens** (of chapter 5), how should a **small firm** internationalize?
8				The **eight rules to follow** to deserve success (conclusion)

1

You can win with ten or lose with a hundred: two examples from the field of war

"Victory belongs to those who make fewer mistakes."

Lord Arwell

1.1 Introduction

THIS CHAPTER EMPLOYS two military examples to show how large armies can lose and small armies can win. The results all depend upon the rules of engagement you follow. We will use two examples from the Zulu War against the British in South Africa. On the morning of 22 January 1879, a British invasion force of over 5000 men was heavily defeated by the Zulu army at Isandlwana. Then in the afternoon of that same day, little more than one hundred British soldiers achieved an astonishing victory at Rorke's Drift.

1.2 The Zulu War[1]

At about 8 p.m. on 22 January 1879, Lieutenant General Lord Chelmsford, the overall commander of the British army, returned to his camp in the vicinity of the Isandlwana mountain. That morning he had ridden out in search of the Zulu army, leaving over 2200 men – a third of his army – back in the camp.

Lord Chelmsford was no fool. He was a career soldier who had taken part in a large number of Victorian military expeditions from Guinea to Abyssinia. His military credentials were impeccable. A few days before, his army of 15,000 men had crossed into Zululand, divided into three columns. He had had months to prepare for a war that he undoubtedly wanted, but which the Zulu King kaMpande had tried at all costs to avoid. Chelmsford's army was highly disciplined, well equipped, and staunchly armed, both with light and heavy firepower. The army was composed of natives, white immigrants, and a large number of regular seasoned British soldiers.

But now, the ruins of his base camp lay before him. Of 2200 men, just 500 survived. The corpses of the rest, including non-fighting civilians, black servants and butlers, along with the bodies of horses, mules, dogs and pets, all lay putrefying under the dying African sun.

The magnitude of the catastrophe was overwhelming. One witness said 'there were no wounded, no missing, only killed'. More officers died at Isandlwana than at Waterloo. And more men were killed than at Inkerman or Alma.

'I can't understand it,' someone overheard the general saying. 'I left two thousand men here.' What happened?

1.3 The path to war

On Christmas Day 1487, the great Portuguese navigator Vasco da Gama gave the name of Natal (Christmas in Portuguese) to the land that stretched north-east from the Cape of Good Hope.[2]

But da Gama's objective was India and so he sailed on. He discovered the route to India and became the first navigator to link Europe and Asia by sea. South Africa was left behind and had to wait a while for Europeans to come to stay. The Dutch were first in 1652, then the British in 1805, inheriting Dutch possessions as a consequence of the Napoleonic wars.

Between the European arrival and the onset of the nineteenth century, the Zulu kingdom grew in strength. Fiercely protective of their independence and organized under a powerful monarchy, the Zulus were located to the north-east of Natal and to the east of the Transvaal (see Figure 1.1).

They first came into contact with the Boers (colonialists of Dutch origin) and then with the English, who used some minor border disputes as a pretext to invade Zululand. Although kaMpande, the Zulu king, tried to negotiate, he would not accept the British conditions ('kaMpande did you no wrong, and I have done you no wrong, therefore you must have some other objective in view in invading my land').[3]

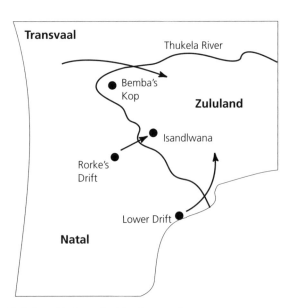

Figure 1.1 ◆ Zululand is invaded in three places

So both sides prepared for war. The Zulu army was an important fighting machine where most warriors had access to some sort of firearm in addition to traditional shields and spears. The 40,000 strong Zulu army also used mounted men as scouts and had defeated neighboring tribes and even the Boers at various times.[4]

Lord Chelmsford's principal fear was that the Zulus would revert to hit-and-run tactics (as the Xhosa had done before), which made it likely that he would not be able to defeat them in a major, decisive battle. So Chelmsford decided to take the initiative and invade the Zulu kingdom using three different columns, each consisting of about 5000 men (see Figure 1.1). The first column was near the coast, from a location called Lower Drift. The second was in the middle, through Rorke's Drift, a small British post. And the third was through Bemba's Kop in the north.

1.4 The invasion

Lord Chelmsford commanded the largest, the most strongly armed, and the most experienced column through Rorke's Drift.

The Zulu king addressed his army close to the capital, Ondini. He told his army that he had no quarrel with the British and that he had not gone overseas to look for them. The British, on the other land, had crossed the seas to confront him. His warriors were indignant. 'Leave the matter with us,' they said. 'The British will not take you while we are alive.'

The King then issued two orders to his generals. First, under no circumstances should they attack a defended British position but attack them in the open. Second, all attacks on the British should be within Zululand. They should drive them back across the border, but on no account cross into Natal themselves.

Late on the afternoon of 17 January 1879, the largest army assembled in the kingdom's history – some 24,000 men – marched out to face the British armies.[5]

The Zulus chose to strike the central column, which under Chelmsford was penetrating fast into the heart of the kingdom. This column had already had a first encounter with a small Zulu army, which at Betshe Valley had taken up a good defensive position. After a fierce but short battle the Zulus were heavily defeated and dispersed. The British moved to a location near Isandlwana Hill and encamped there.

1.5 The battle of Isandlwana

Historians disagree on minor details of what happened next. But the accepted outline is as follows.

1   Although his war orders insisted that all permanent camps should be partially entrenched, Lord Chelmsford did not try to protect the camp. Later he argued that the camp was too large and the ground too rocky to excavate trenches all around it (see Figure 1.2(a)).

   Besides, Chelmsford expected to move on within a day or two. So no attempt was made to even form a barricade of thorn bush, much less a circle of wagons. As a result, all that was preventing the Zulus from charging was the British firepower.

2   For the first day the Zulus remained out of sight. Chelmsford despatched about a third of his 5000 men under the command of Major Dartwell to look for the Zulu army (see Figure 1.2(b)).

3   With the exception of small parties of Zulus that appeared and disappeared, refusing to engage, Major Dartwell found the country free of large bodies of the enemy. So he pressed on, sweeping the hills and reconnoitering the terrain.

4   About 12 miles away from the base camp, however, an army of 1000 warriors suddenly appeared. They blocked Dartwell's way and took their traditional battle formation: a half-circle in the form of chest and horns of a bull (see Figure 1.2(c)).

5   Unsure how many more Zulus might be in the area, Major Dartwell decided not to engage the enemy, but instead opted to bivouac where he was for the night and asked Lord Chelmsford to reinforce him.

6   Lord Chelmsford received the message at 2 a.m. The encounter he had been expecting for days was apparently about to happen. So at dawn he marched out of the camp (see Figure 1.2(c)).

7   He left the base camp under the leadership of Lieutenant-Colonel Pulleine with over 1700 men, soon reinforced by another 500 from the frontier post of Rorke's Drift, giving a total of nearly 2200 men at the base camp.

8   After Lord Chelmsford's departure, scouts reported parties of Zulus nearby. Moreover, small groups of Zulus had let themselves be seen from the base camp. Some were apparently driving cattle.

9 Fearing that the Zulus on the hills intended to cut off Chelmsford from the camp, 500 British rode out of the camp under the command of Colonel Durnford (see Figure 1.2(d)).

10 Four miles from the camp they saw a small party of Zulus who appeared to be trying to escape and who suddenly disappeared into a fold in the ground. The British cantered up behind them.

11 Suddenly, in front of them was a steep slope dropping into a narrow valley. At the bottom of this was the main Zulu army: more than 20,000 strong! To remain undetected it had lit no fires and waited in silence.

12 Within minutes, the whole Zulu army was on the move and formed their traditional chest and horns half-circle battle position.

13 The British immediately withdrew the way they had come. They performed one of the most difficult military manoeuvers: a controlled retreat. The soldiers would withdraw; then halt and deliver a volley; then retire again (see Figure 1.2(e)).[6]

14 Back at base camp, Commander Pulleine was still unaware of the extent of the danger. He could see Durnford's men retreating fast across the plain. But he still believed that the real danger was 12 miles away with Chelmsford and Dartwell. So instead of taking immediate defensive measures, he sent some of his men to help the retreat of Colonel Durnford (see Figure 1.2(f)).

15 Reinforced from the base camp, Durnford decided to make a stand as the Zulus got closer, who responded by alternately rushing forward and then throwing themselves down into the grass to escape the British fire.

16 As more Zulus came over the hill, Pulleine sent his men forward to form a slightly bent line, facing north with the camp in the rear. The line was over-extended, so there were considerable gaps among the units (see Figure 1.2(g)).

17 By now, the Zulus were massing heavily on the British. Their half-circle formation enabled them both to penetrate through the gaps and to outflank the British defense line. Furthermore, with his men beginning to run out of ammunition, Durnford's position became untenable and he ordered his men to fall back on the camp (see Figure 1.2(h)).

(a) The British establish their base   (b) With the Zulus out of sight,
     camp and do not entrench it.   Major Dartwell leaves the
     The Zulu army stays in hiding   camp looking for them

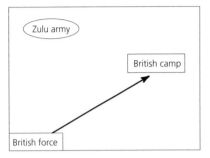   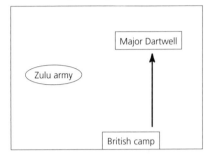

(c) A force of 1000 Zulus confronts   (d) The Zulus lure a third force (led
     but does not engage Major Dartwell   by Colonel Durnford) out of the
     who asks for and obtains   base camp
     reinforcements from Lord Chelmsford

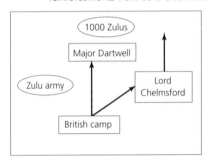   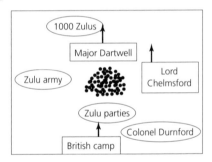

(e) Colonel Durnford finds the Zulu army, and begins retreating
     in the face of the Zulus who rapidly form in the traditional
     battle position of chest and horn

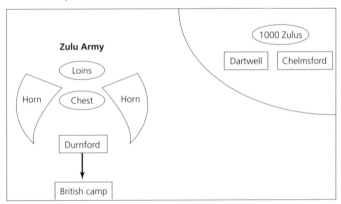

Figure 1.2 ◆ The phases of the Isandlwana battle

(f) The camp commander Pulleine tries to help Durnford and sends
some reinforcements

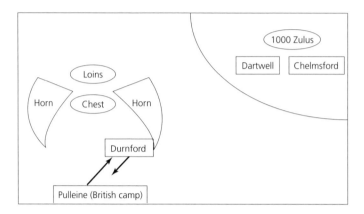

(g) Pulleine sends his men forward forming a slightly bent line
facing north

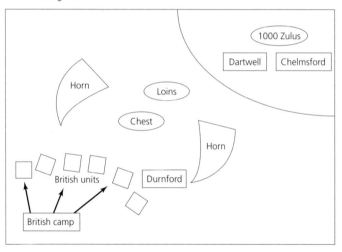

(h)   The Zulus penetrate through the gaps and start to encircle the British line. Ammunition starts running short

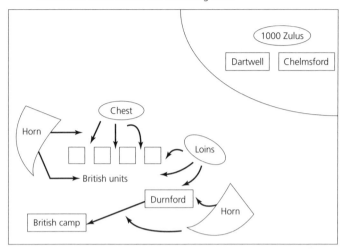

(i)   Finally perceiving he faces a major battle, Pulleine orders a general retreat into the base camp. Under Zulu pressure this is not done well. Some soldiers drop their weapons and run. At the base camp the British do not offer a single formation but reply in separate groups

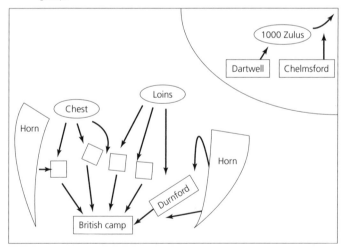

(j)   The Zulus encircle, besiege, and then annihilate the separate
      British units at the base camp. Fewer than 500 soldiers
      manage to escape

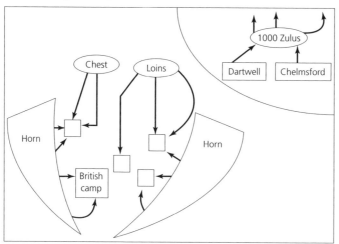

18   Only now did Pulleine realize that he had a major battle on his hands.
     He decided to call back his men, fall back on the tents, and try to
     present a solid formation in the base camp (see Figure 1.2(i)).

     Twelve miles away, Major Dartwell and Lord Chelmsford were still
     trying to hunt down the Zulu party of 1000 men that by now had
     managed to escape.

19   Some of the men were able to retreat to the tents. Others threw down
     their weapons and ran for the rear. There was no time to offer the
     attacking Zulus a strong defensive position. Gaps were everywhere and it
     was difficult to rally the British soldiers. Thus, rather than an organized,
     unified and single formation, the soldiers rallied in squares, dispersed
     into the field, and were cut off from each other. The encircling Zulus
     systematically began to wipe them out (see Figure 1.2(j)).

20   Horror reigned in the camp's last moments. Stabbed, speared, and
     gunned down, the British soldiers fell in the field, within the tents, by
     the wagons, and even in shallow caves near the summit of Isandlwana.

     For the most part the British stood and fought, angry and adamant
     to the very end. A few, however, presumably colonialists, called out in
     Zulu, begging to be spared. The Zulus replied, 'How can we give you
     mercy when you want to take away our country?' and killed them.

Organized resistance was over at about 2 p.m., although some groups resisted until late afternoon. After the fighting the Zulus vented their anger and fury on the camp. Following custom, they slit their victims' stomachs to allow their spirit to escape to after life. As in lion hunts, the bodies were stabbed again and again by passing warriors. Maddened warriors slashed, hacked and mutilated hundreds of corpses.

With the exception of some transport oxen, which were driven off, everything in the camp was killed. Tents were burnt. Boxes of supplies were cast open and spread in the field. On the Zulu side, 1000 warriors were killed and the same number badly wounded. Then, carrying their wounded, the Zulu army began slowly drifting away.

A few British men did manage to escape across the river, which marked the frontier between Zululand and Natal. But of the 2200 in the base camp that morning, less than 60 whites and 400 blacks were alive at sunset.

1.6 Rorke's Drift temptation

Mindful of their king's orders, most Zulus did not cross the frontier into Natal. However, a body of 4000 warriors commanded by the king's brother had played a secondary role during the battle. They wanted to receive the glory of the Zulus who had been more active. A few miles away, a hundred or so British soldiers defended the frontier post of Rorke's Drift. The odds were nearly forty to one. So the Zulus decided to attack it.

1.7 The battle of Rorke's Drift

Rorke's Drift had been built by a trader named James Rorke and was requisitioned by Lord Chelmsford at the beginning of the war to use as a hospital and a supply depot. News of the approaching Zulu army had led to the defection of several soldiers and native helpers. Those fleeing Isandlwana stopped briefly to give the news and then moved on hastily.

A total of 138 men remained, of which 97 were healthy soldiers. Seventeen belonged to an engineering unit repairing bridges on the nearby river and 80 were infantrymen. Of the remaining men, four were hospital staff and 37 were hospital patients.

Lieutenant Chard, from the Royal Engineers, was of senior rank to Lieutenant Bromhead from the infantry so Chard took charge. Using the available wagons, biscuits and mealie sacks, he connected the three buildings (church, hospital and warehouse) and created an entrenched positioned with an outer and an inner wall. This was the redoubt where the last stand was to be made (see Figure 1.3).

Lieutenant Chard distributed guns to the sick in the hospital, ordered all those who could stand to join the other soldiers on the outside walls and posted two vigils on a nearby hill.

He did not have long to wait. There was the noise of feet running rhythmically. The vigils reported 'Zulus; from the northeast; by the thousands'. And a little later, drawing a line in the horizon across the field, the Zulu army allowed itself to be seen.

The first move by the Zulus was to place shooters on the nearby hill, some of them with rifles obtained at Isandlwana. From here they targeted the British soldiers at the walls. Chard gave orders for the soldiers in the confronting wall to respond to the fire. This fire exchange continued for most of the ensuing battle.

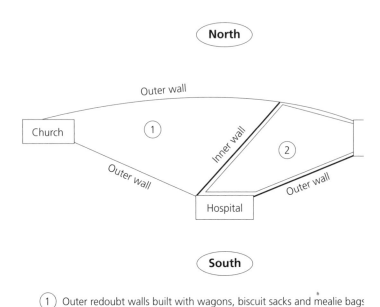

① Outer redoubt walls built with wagons, biscuit sacks and mealie bags

② Inner redoubt (same)

Figure 1.3 ◆ The British entrenchment at Rorke's Drift

(a) **First phase:** The Zulus attack and are stopped at the north wall

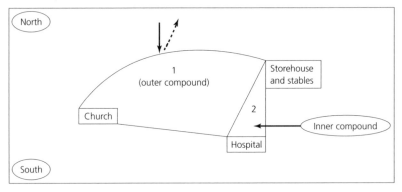

(b) **Second phase:** The Zulus attack and are defeated at the south wall

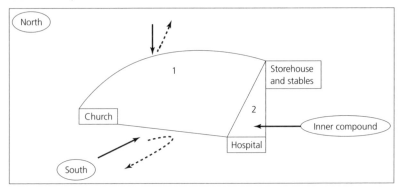

(c) **Third phase:** The Zulus again attack the north wall and force the British to flee to the inner compound, where they compel the Zulus to retreat

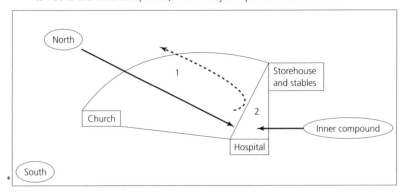

Figure 1.4 ◆ The phases of the battle of Rorke's Drift

(d) Fourth phase: The Zulus for the first time attack two walls simultaneously: the north and the hospital. The hospital and the storehouse are burnt down. Resistance at the inner compound (2), together with trampliing by a herd of oxon, defeat the attack

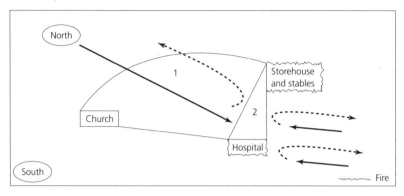

(e) Fifth phase: The Zulus simultaneously attack the north and south walls and force the British to retreat to the inner compound (2) where they resist all night long

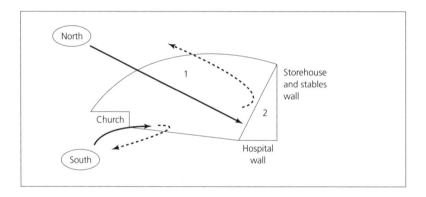

The next move by the Zulus was to send hundreds of warriors charging to within a few dozen meters of the British line. Here they started shouting and beating their spears on their shields and dancing. Volley after volley of British fire came upon them but they did not budge: they were testing the British fire-power for the Zulu's commander, Prince Dabulamanzi, to evaluate. Once he had done so he ordered his warriors to withdraw.

The Zulus were finally ready to engage and charge the British lines. They made five different attacks. The first on the north wall was halted after a hand-to-hand fight (see Figure 1.4(a)). The Zulus withdrew. The next attack came upon the south wall (see Figure 1.4(b)), with the British managing to stop the Zulus at the outer wall. Zulu survivors fled.

A third charge was launched against the longer north wall. When it was about to be overtaken, the British commander gave orders for the soldiers to withdraw to the inner wall, separating the redoubts (see Figure 1.4(c)). At the inner wall, some soldiers kneeled at the outside while others stood in the inner side. Each group fired alternately at the Zulus until they fled, leaving hundreds of dead and wounded in the compound.

With darkness came a fourth attack, now on the hospital side. The Zulus managed to take the hospital through a hole in the wall and climbed into the roof before the hospital and storehouse buildings were burned to the ground, leaving the ruins of a standing wall as sole protection against the outside (see Figure 1.4(d)).

At the same time, the Zulus attacked the north wall, which fell. The surviving soldiers withdrew to the interior redoubt (see Figure 1.4(e)). As a last resort, they set free a herd of oxen from the stables, which trampled the attacking Zulus and forced them to retreat.

A fifth attack was then made on both the north and south outer walls simultaneously (see Figure 1.4(e)). After long resistance, the British fled to the inner wall. Here soldiers both in front and behind the wall fired alternately on the Zulu advance.

The British were now concentrated on a very small front and the combined effect of firepower and bayonets kept the Zulus back, despite repeated attacks that lasted most of the night. About an hour before dawn the Zulu fire dwindled and they escaped into the darkness (see Figure 1.4(e)).

The British cared for the wounded, rested and waited for another attack, but none came. Daylight showed a scene of devastation. Only the church remained standing. A curtain of smoke lay over the field. The dead were everywhere: a few British soldiers, but mostly Zulus, sometimes piled up to the top of the barricade. As the morning developed, so did the certainty that the Zulus had withdrawn.

1.7.1 Why did the Zulus go?

They had been on the move since Colonel Durnford's men first discovered them at the start of the Isandlwana battle, 24 hours earlier. They had run over 15 miles of rugged country. They had fought throughout the previous afternoon and all through the night. They were hungry and their enemy was as entrenched as ever. From their position they could see Lord Chelmsford approaching from the direction of Isandlwana. In addition, they had lost heavily: 600 dead and 400 wounded, an extraordinary casualty rate of nearly one in four. So they withdrew. Ninety-seven soldiers, 37 patients, and four medical staff had won the day against an enemy of 4000.

The British victory at Rorke's Drift was extraordinary by all accounts, in terms of bravery, importance in the ensuing war, and how it was obtained against all odds.

1.7.2 Bravery

In over a century the Victoria Cross (Britain's highest award for bravery in action) had been given to just 1344 men. At Rorke's Drift, 13 of the British soldiers received it (two of these posthumously).

1.7.3 Importance

The victory at Rorke's Drift may have weakened the Zulus' resolve to cross into Natal and pursue their victory at Isandlwana; so it may have saved thousands of lives on the British side. It gave time for Lord Chelmsford to regroup his forces and to reorganize the north and south columns, who would soon encounter the Zulus. And it enabled him to plan a second invasion, which would finally defeat Zulu King kaMpande.

1.8 Conclusion

The victory at Rorke's Drift was remarkable since the British army faced greater obstacles than the expedition at Isandlwana:

- ◆ *Numbers*: at Rorke's Drift 100 British faced 4000 Zulu warriors. At Isandlwana 5000 British faced 24,000 Zulus; a much higher proportion.

- ◆ *Morale*: in 1879 the British army was the backbone of an expanding empire. Morale being high, defeat in Zululand was not a serious consideration in the minds of seasoned British soldiers. Their main problem (they thought) would be to pin the Zulu army down and oblige it to fight. At Rorke's Drift, morale was understandably low.

Survivors from Isandlwana streamed past in retreat, shouted at the Rorke's Drift garrison that they had had enough and rode off. The sight was even too much for some of the Rorke's Drift troops, who also vaulted the barricades and fled after them.

◆ *Training*: Rorke's Drift acted as a makeshift hospital and depot. Seventeen of the soldiers who fought at Rorke's Drift belonged to an engineering unit repairing a bridge. Four others included a surgeon and three hospital orderlies. Then there were 37 patients. Only 80 regular infantry soldiers guarded the post.

◆ *Leadership*: as Rorke's Drift was an outpost, the officer in charge, Lieutenant Bromhead, had neither the rank nor the experience of the leaders at Isandlwana. Under attack, Lieutenant Chard of the engineering unit assumed command as he outranked Bromhead. It was Chard's first battle.

◆ *Technology*: the British at Isandlwana had several pieces of artillery and rifles superior to those of the Zulus. But at Rorke's Drift, the British garrison possessed no artillery whatsoever and faced Zulus equipped with their own rifles, collected from the dead at Isandlwana. While at Isandlwana the British technology was superior, at Rorke's Drift it was more even.

From the British standpoint, the numbers, morale, training, leadership, and technology were much more favorable at Isandlwana than at Rorke's Drift. But they lost the former and won the latter. Why? We will discuss the reasons in the next chapter.

2

The reasons for victory and defeat – and the lessons for business

"We learn how to win when defeated."

Simon Bolivar

2.1 Introduction

WHY WERE THE RESULTS at Isandlwana and Rorke's Drift precisely the opposite of what one would expect?

At Rorke's Drift the British made the correct tactical decisions while the Zulus made mistakes. At Isandlwana, the roles were reversed: the Zulus were in the right and the British made the mistakes. Those decisions and mistakes can be summarized as four variables:

◆ Knowledge of the enemy (characteristics and plans).

◆ Focus.

◆ Choice of terrain.

◆ Surprise.

2.2 Knowledge of the enemy's characteristics and plans

From the start of the war, the British army misunderstood the objectives of the Zulus. Remembering his experience with other African tribes such as the Xhosa, Chelmsford was convinced that his main problem would be trying to avoid a guerrilla war of hit-and-run tactics. He was determined to pin the Zulu army down and force it to engage in major battle.

At Isandlwana his major concern was to look for the enemy (not prepare to fight them). Even 12 miles away he was chasing a non-existent Zulu army. When he received information that a major battle was taking place at the base camp, he was sceptical. After all, he had left 2200 men behind. What was there to worry about?

Chelmsford reckoned that the Zulus feared the British and would never engage in an all-or-nothing battle. So, since the Zulus would not come to him, he would have to go to them. He could not have been more wrong.

He was right to the extent that the Zulus frequently fought like other African tribes. There had been guerrilla wars with the Dutch, then the Boers, and finally the British, and battles with a strong ritualistic content with other African tribes.

Opposing armies would meet at an appointed place and time and open the proceedings by taunting each other. Moral superiority was the key to victory rather than killing the enemy, since one side usually backed down before casualties became too heavy.

Shaka, Zulu king from 1817 to 1820 changed all that. He modified both the weapons and the tactics. The objective now was to come into contact with the enemy as quickly as possible. He also developed a tactic known as 'Impondo Zankomo' (the beast's horns), composed of six basic steps (see Figure 2.1):

1 The army would be divided in four like a buffalo's body: two horns in the wings; a third section in the centre (the chest), and a fourth section (loins) behind (Figure 2.1(a)).

2 In battle, the central body would rush down to the enemy, which would naturally advance to meet it (Figure 2.1(b)).

3 After a light skirmish the central section would first withdraw, tempting the enemy to follow (Figure 2.1(c)).

4 The central section would then split in two to reinforce the wings (Figure 2.1(d)).

5 The fourth section (loins) would then move forward to halt the enemy's advance (Figure 2.1(e)).

6 The two horn sections would then encircle the enemy from behind (Figure 2.1(f)).

Most adversaries would soon crumble under such a sophisticated and brilliant tactic. As traditional Zulu enemies it's likely that the Boers in Chelmsford's army would have warned him of it. But Chelmsford was convinced the Zulus would rely on guerrilla tactics.

The Zulus knew the British army well from past experiences at the battle of Thukela and Blood River in 1838 and Ndohdakusuka in 1856. So King kaMpande strongly advised his departing army not to attack defended positions, but to catch the British in the open.

But Chelmsford was right to the extent that the Zulus were cautious because of their fear of British power. Even after the major victory at Isandlwana there were no Zulu invasions into Natal or Transvaal. Until Rorke's Drift, the Zulus always opted for moderation and always fought a defensive war.

The Zulus understood the British much better than the British understood the Zulus. As Sun Tzu says in *The Art of War*, it is a great strength 'to understand our enemy better than he understands us. Regardless of how weak we are in the first place.'

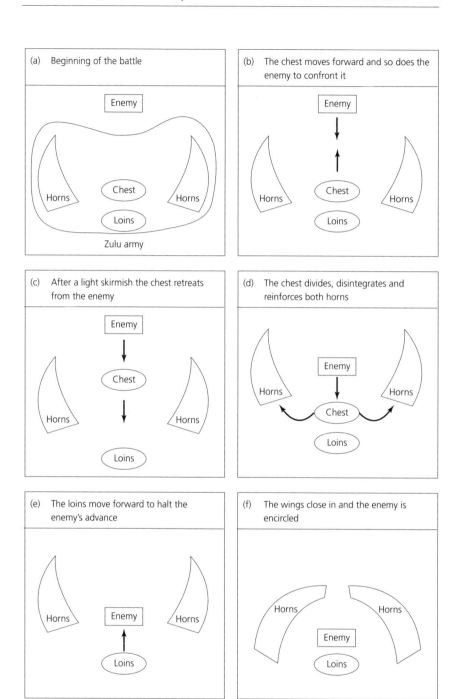

Figure 2.1 ◆ The Zulu tactic of the beast's horns (Impondo Zankomo)

At Rorke's Drift the roles were reversed. In the aftermath of the Isandlwana slaughter, the British knew that the Zulus had already dared to attack a
British army. They also knew that a battle in open field was tantamount to disaster because of the disproportion in numbers, the high grass and slopes in
the terrain that allowed the Zulus to hide from the British firepower, and the
mobility of the Zulu army.

When faced with the options of staying put and fighting, or fleeing and
risking being caught in the open, the garrison opted for barricading themselves in. Fighting the enemy from an entrenched position maximized the
power of their concentrated fire.

Ironically, the Zulus now made the mistakes that the British had made at
Isandlwana. Commanded by the headstrong and aggressive prince Dabulamanzi, brother of the king, they disregarded first the king's order not to attack
the British in an entrenched position. They also ignored the fact that the terrain around Rorke's Drift post lacked the high grass and slopes that protected
the Zulus at Isandlwana.

Thus, in spite of their strength in numbers the Zulus became targets for
the British. The result was a disaster.

Knowledge of the enemy is also fundamental in business. Competitor
intelligence centres on two areas. First, know the *plans* (i.e. the objectives) of
the competitors. Then know their *characteristics* (strengths and weaknesses).

This intelligence enables a firm to decide strategy (i.e. which segments to
compete in), tactics (how to compete in the selected segments – i.e. the marketing, production and finance plans), and time (when to compete) (see Figure 2.2 for an analysis of this).

An example of how competitor information is important to make *strategic
decisions* is provided by Hewlett Packard. HP understood the strategy of a
major competitor: Texas Instruments. Texas based its strategy and manufacturing operations on the economics of the experience curve and priced and
marketed its products accordingly. The company would cut prices aggressively in anticipation of the volume benefits of learning-curve economics.

In retaliation Hewlett-Packard kept away from the central segment of the
industry and made high-quality products at premium prices instead, such as
the scientific calculator.

By understanding Texas's strategy, Hewlett-Packard was able to pull itself
from a major confrontation where it would be worse off.[1]

Procter & Gamble's difficulties with Pringles illustrates how competitor
intelligence is useful for *tactical decisions* – i.e. to decide *how* to compete.

Competitor intelligence Utility	Areas of information	Competitors	
		Plans (objectives)	**Characteristics** (Strengths and weaknesses)
Where to compete (strategy)		✓	✓
How to compete (tactics)		✓	✓
When to compete (time)		✓	✓
Key: ✓ indicates what a given area of information can be used for			

Figure 2.2 ◆ Analysis of competitor intelligence

Pringles snack food was formulated and designed carefully and was launched with the heavy support of P&G promotion, distribution and finance. P&G hoped it would attack the ground held by Frito Lay and Wise. The latter invested in market research to determine what customers disliked about Pringles – the answers turned out to be lack of natural ingredients and taste. Frito Lay and Wise then produced a flavour and natural ingredient campaign that gave Pringles difficulties in the marketplace.

The lesson is the value of knowing the strengths and weaknesses of your competitor's products. If your product is superior in taste, color, performance, shape, ease of handling, size, precision or any other quality that demonstrates its superiority – make lots of noise about it.

How common is this competitor intelligence analysis in business? Not very. As Michael Porter put it, 'Most firms don't examine their competitors in any depth. They make a list of their strengths and weaknesses but don't really understand the motivations and their competitor's behaviour.'[2]

How serious is this drawback? Since intelligence and operations are interdependent, 'the degree of success achieved by any unit in accomplishing its mission will be directly affected by the intelligence which it develops and uses, and the manner in which it is used.'[3]

Indeed, as Sun Tzu emphasized as long ago as the fourth century BC, meticulous planning based upon sound intelligence is the key to victory:

Know the enemy and know yourself; in a hundred battles you will never be in peril. When you are ignorant of the enemy but know yourself, your chances of winning or losing are equal. If ignorant both of your enemy and of yourself, you are certain in every battle to be in peril.[4]

2.3 Focus

The Zulus achieved greater focus than their opponents (see Figure 2.3). At the start of the war the British invasion army had over 15,000 men (leaving aside the black border police and other defensive units in Natal and Transvaal). The Zulu army had a total of 40,000 men. King kaMpande divided his army into two major groups: 16,000 warriors were scattered around the kingdom in defensive positions and 24,000 constituted the striking force. So he decreased his battle strength from 40,000 to 24,000 – 40 percent.

Chelmsford divided his army into three columns of 5000 men. So, when commanding the central column, his battle strength had been lowered by 66 percent (from 15,000 to 5000 men). At Isandlwana the relative strength of

Phase	Relative strength	Cause
I Beginning of the war	15^1:40 (1:2.6)	Population
II Chelmsford arrives at Isandlwana	5:24 (1:5)	British misjudgement of Zulu intentions
III Zulus attack	2.2^2:24 (1:11)	Zulus' ruse

1 Plus defensive forces
2 Of which 500 headed by Colonel Durnford were separated from the rest of the forces by a mile or more

Figure 2.3 ◆ Evolution of the relative strengths of the British against the Zulu army until the defeat of Isandlwana

the British in the face of the Zulus had changed from 1:2.6 (15,000 against 40,000) at the beginning of the war, to nearly 1:5 (5000 against 24,000).

Until that point the Zulus had been able to maintain higher concentration and focus than the British. Another factor further diluted the focus of the British army – the Zulus' ruses. First they attracted Dartwell away from the base camp, then Chelmsford, and finally Durnford.

Consequently, when the army attacked they found it defended by only 2200 and not 5000, and Durnford's forces were at a considerable distance from the rest of the army located at the base camp. The ultimate result was a strength ratio of 1:11.

At Rorke's Drift, the situation was reversed. The British opted for concentration, building first an exterior wall connecting the buildings and then an interior wall where they held out successfully against the last two Zulu attacks.

The Zulus did not focus as well as they could have done, for two reasons. First, they did not immediately send their 4000 warriors in a single attack against the British garrison. Instead they made five different attacks, each with between 500 and 1000 warriors. They probably feared that too many warriors in a narrow front would do more harm than good, with some getting in the way of the others and thus affecting the mobility of all.

Second, only in the final attacks did the Zulus strike simultaneously at two or more walls. In the first three charges they attacked only one wall at a time, opting to shoot at the soldiers in the other walls from the hill nearby. They feared, and with some reason, that if they kept shooting and attacking several walls at the same time they would end up accidentally killing their own warriors.

This choice proved to be a mistake since the Zulus' skills with firearms were no match for the British. A better tactic for the Zulus would have been to avoid long-range shootouts and instead attack several walls simultaneously.

At Isandlwana the Zulus achieved higher focus than the British. But at Rorke's Drift the British concentrated their forces better. In warfare and business, few things are as important as focus. Lessons for business come from antiquity and the military.

Confucius said, 'A man who chases two rabbits catches neither.' Later Archimedes said, 'give me somewhere to stand, and I will move the earth.'

Carl von Clausewitz said, 'In war few things are as important as placing one's army so that instead of being weak in many places, it is strong in few.' Ferdinand Foch said, 'He who defends everything, defends nothing.' And, finally, in Mao Tse-tung's words, 'I have ten against one hundred, but I always attack ten against one, one hundred times. That way I win.'

In business the same principle applies. Peter F. Drucker said, 'the difference between successful and unsuccessful diversified companies is that the former have a core of unity, be it technology or market.' In Al Ries' words, 'Instead of expanding, companies should go the opposite direction. They should get back to basics. They should focus.'

Focus – or its absence – is the reason suggested for the decaying dominant role IBM has played in the computer industry.

IBM began by manufacturing typewriters. In the 1940s IBM developed huge computers (the so-called super computers) for the army. Later in the 1950s, it performed a successful frontal attack on Univac, which had pioneered mainframes. Then in a fourth phase IBM grew to cover all major segments of the computer industry (hardware, software and support services) with great success. This led some analysts to say that within the computer industry, IBM was not a competitor but the environment itself. Others designated IBM's competitors as the BUNCH: Burroughs, Univac, NCR, Control Data, and Honeywell. Of the BUNCH only NCR stayed profitable up to the late 1980s but it was finally taken over by AT&T. This conglomerate was to lose billions of dollars in the US computer business.

A fifth phase started at the end of the 1970s when IBM crossed the boundaries of the computer industry and moved into other areas related to information processing – photocopiers, satellite equipment, telephone equipment, etc.

The last phase of this defocussing expansion path came when IBM added ancillary services such as strategic consulting, e-business, technical and professional training, and financing.

IBM's six gradually defocussing stages are summarized in Figure 2.4. In his book *Focus*,[5] Al Ries demonstrates that IBM, despite being a huge corporation by any standards (sales of over $88 billion in 2000), started to unravel by losing focus. Instead of following Peter Drucker's advice to 'apply scarce resources to the greatest opportunities' IBM stretched its resources too thinly. The result?

◆ *Battles lost*: In the 1980s IBM tried to take Xerox's dominance of the copier industry away – and failed.

◆ *Money squandered*: In the early 1990s, IBM suffered year after year of losses. In the first three years of the decade this amounted to $16.5 billion dollars.[6]

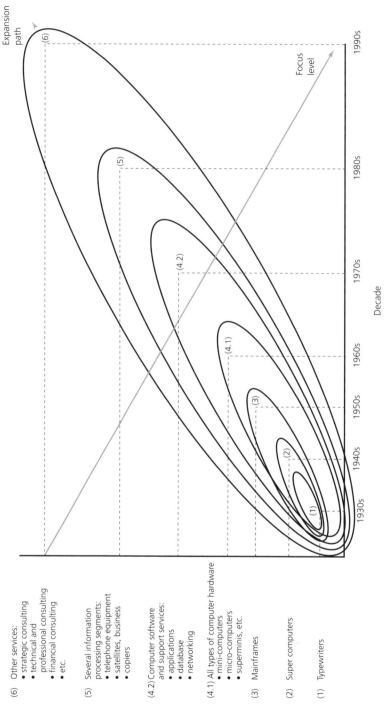

Figure 2.4 ◆ IBM's unfocussed expansion: (1) typewriters; (2) supercomputers; (3) mainframes; (4) mini-computers, superminis and micro-computers, plus hardware, software and support services; (5) information processing; (6) ancillary business (consulting, etc.)

◆ *Businesses sold*: Copiers to Kodak, telephone equipment to Siemens, satellite equipment to MCI, etc. The company also managed to let Microsoft and Intel outgrow and out-profit IBM. How did they achieve this? By being specialists – instead of the generalist that IBM became. They concentrated their strength at a single decisive point (the market segment that they decided had the greatest potential opportunities for them) instead of trying to cover the ground that IBM spread itself over.

So IBM is a perfect illustration of the proverb, 'You can win with ten and lose with a hundred.'

In the 1950s, IBM followed a more sensible path. It launched a me-too mainframe against Remington Rand. Market leader Remington Rand supplied large business organizations, whereas IBM was a super computer specialist, serving the army niche.

IBM was able to conquer the mainframe segment even though Remington Rand had had a head start in the business in the 1950s. IBM succeeded because of its strengths in two key areas: software and servicing (installation, training and maintenance).

Forty years later, the story was to be reversed. Although much larger, IBM lost the software battle to Microsoft. IBM also became prey to other specialists who decided to join the struggle: the prize was a piece of IBM's market.

IBM's story can be divided into two phases:

◆ *Phase I – Growth*: Although a small company, IBM successfully took on not only Remington Rand but also conglomerates as large as AT&T and General Electric. It also embarrassed European competitors such as Olivetti in Italy, ICL in England, and Bull in France. It pushed PC specialist Tandy into oblivion, created problems for word processor specialist Wang, and put Kaypro out of business. At the end of IBM's period of growth, only the large Japanese firms prospered.[7]

◆ *Phase 2 – Decline*: This started when Microsoft snatched the software PC market. Then by refusing to sacrifice any segment of the computer field, IBM became an attractive target for all types of specialists: PC specialists (Compaq, Packard, Bell, Gateway, Dell); workstation specialists (Sun, Hewlett-Packard, Silicon Graphics); and software specialists (Microsoft, Oracle, Novell, Lotus).[8] By the late 1990s, Microsoft's stock was worth more than GM's, despite being one twentieth of the size.

By the early 1990s IBM had lost $75 billion of stock-market value, was forced to write off $20 billion of assets, and decreased its workforce from 407,000 in 1986 to 260,000 in 1994.[9]

Defocussing shows why 'to think is to say no', in the words of A. Alain. The most important word in strategy is 'no'. Instead of asking, 'which segments, industries and geographical areas shall I be present in?' the question to ask is 'which shall I stay away from?'

Getting this question wrong has been the problem for many companies that have seemed to be afflicted by an attention deficit disorder (Chrysler, AT&T, Eastman Kodak, even Playboy).[10] They don't stay focussed. Instead of doing a few things well, they end up doing many things poorly. They grow weaker, not stronger, and they see their multiple enemies outpace them.

Companies like Cray computers, BMW, and Cooper Tires & Rubbers prove that a company grows by staying focussed. Getting diversification right can also prove successful – Gerber and Taneba and Coca Cola prove as much. How to diversify or focus well is covered in later chapters.

2.4 Choice of terrain

This is the third explanation for the different outcomes at Isandlwana and Rorke's Drift.

At Isandlwana, the Zulus had three environmental elements in their favor. First, high grass which enabled the attacking warriors to rush forward and then throw themselves down into the grass to conceal them from British firepower.

Second, slopes. Even a few miles from the British base camp the slopes prevented Pulleine from realizing that the Zulu army was closing in until it was too late. Neither grass nor slopes were present at the battle of Nyezane where the British decisively defeated the Zulus.

Third, artificial barriers. At Isandlwana there were no laagers or barricaded circles of wagons, as were used by the Boers and then successfully by the British at Khambula and Gingindlovu. There was not even a simple barricade of thorn bush.

At Rorke's Drift, the lack of high grass and slopes enabled the British to see the Zulu movements in advance, hundreds of meters away.

The Zulus needed to reach close quarters with the enemy for their tactics to work, because although they outnumbered the British, their firepower was inferior. The terrain of Isandlwana allowed the Zulus to reach the British without them noticing. The situation at Rorke's Drift's did not allow this.

The argument regarding the choice of terrain can be summarized in five major points:

1 The threefold strengths of the Zulu armies:
   1.1 numbers (superior to the English);
   1.2 mobility (in battles and covering long distances between them); and
   1.3 weaponry adequate for hand-to-hand combat.

2 The Zulus' weakness was inferior firepower: older generation rifles and lack of heavy artillery.

3 Zulu strengths were maximized and weaknesses minimized in combat at close quarters.

4 To attain this close-quarters combat, the terrain had to have:
   4.1 high grass; and/or
   4.2 slopes; and/or
   4.3 no British entrenchment (laager-barricaded circle of wagons, buildings, and other artificial barriers)

5 If grass and slopes were present and there were no artificial barriers, the Zulus' strengths were maximized and their weaknesses minimized.

Figure 2.5 illustrates this.

It is crucial to choose a terrain with favorable characteristics in business, too. Pizza Hut was an early entrant in the pizza restaurant category outside continental Europe, and had the luxury of several competitive advantages: strong positioning in the mind of the customer as 'the' pizza company; experience of an 'across the board' menu based on a suppliers' network that guaranteed high quality; and a large retail chain to spread overheads.

So did number two and number three pizza chains take Pizza Hut head on? No. Number two company, Little Caesars, focussed on takeaways. Number three, Domino's, focussed on home delivery. The slogan of Little Caesars is 'Two pizzas for the price of one.' The slogan of Domino's is: 'Home delivery in thirty minutes, guaranteed.' The results? Little Caesars has 35 percent of the take-out segment and Domino's has 40 percent of the home delivery.[11]

In a scene in *Raiders of the Lost Ark*, Indiana Jones is confronted in a Cairo street by a huge black-hooded, scimitar-twirling opponent. What did Indy do? He assessed the situation, retreated a few steps, nonchalantly pulled a pistol from his belt, and shot his assailant. Indiana Jones saw that if he were to

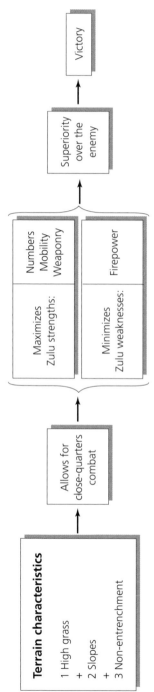

Figure 2.5 ◆ Choice of terrain

fight the thug on his own terms (with a scimitar, spear, etc.) the chances are he would lose. So, he changed the terms of engagement to suit his strengths instead of the opponent's. He changed the nature of the battle so that he had a competitive advantage.

Examples from other industries transmit the same message: choose a terrain adequate to your strengths. Choose your conditions. Change the terms of engagement.

Federal Express provides another good example. Established in 1973, it had its own planes and trucks and a unique hub-and-spoke distribution system based in Memphis, Tennessee. Federal Express's strategy was to sell a better service at a cheaper price, focussing on heavy packages. The main competitor was Emery Air Freight, the largest and most profitable company in the industry.

Federal Express did not, however, possess the required strengths to be cheaper. Besides, it's hard to be cheaper when you also want to be better. So, Federal Express decided to fight in another terrain – not in price, convenience, or size of the packages, but in *speed*. Federal Express focussed the company on its overnight service. Priority three (three-day delivery) was dropped.[12]

Naturally, advertising was also changed to implement this main strategy. It focussed on executives rather than mailroom supervisors and carried a new slogan: 'When it absolutely, positively, has to be overnight.' Any mention of being *cheaper* was left out. So 'overnight' became the new battlecry at Federal Express, and it turned the company around. It broke even in 1975, went public in 1978 at $25 a share, and three years later that share was worth $180. By 1980, profits were over $50 million annually.

When Federal Express shifted its strategy from 'better and cheaper' to emphasize 'overnight' it allowed its prices to increase higher than the competition's. The company made more money, the money enabled it to improve its services further and the better service reinforced its reputation. A virtuous circle.

Fight where it suits you. Choose the terms of engagement. Rely on your strengths. Choose the nature of the battleground and the kind of terrain you will fight on. That has always been the recipe for success.

2.5 Surprise

Surprise also played an important role in the outcome of both battles. At Rorke's Drift the benefit of surprise was with the British if it was anywhere. The Zulus faced an enemy in a strong position instead of a fleeing enemy in the open field that would have been easy to prey upon.

The British faced no unexpected events. They had received warning from soldiers fleeing Isandlwana that the Zulus were coming. They knew their numbers, so were psychologically prepared. And they had last-minute warnings given by two sentinels they placed on the top of the nearby hill.

But at Isandlwana the British faced one surprise after the other. Dartwell thought he was facing the main Zulu army, when he was confronted merely by a war party consisting of 1000 men. Chelmsford thought the enemy was 12 miles away from the base camp. Durnford, pursuing enemy patrols, literally bumped into the Zulu army. At base camp, even after the shooting began, Pulleine didn't think he was facing the main Zulu army until it was too late (Figure 1.2(i), Chapter 1).

In business, surprise ought to be an important element of any attack, for two reasons. First, the greater the surprise, the longer it will take the competitor to react and try to recover. The most successful moves are the ones that are completely unexpected.

Second, surprise also *demoralizes* the competition. Top management is tongue-tied. The sales force, PR department and Personnel are all muted. A classic example of the importance of surprise is the case of Datril of Bristol-Myers against Tylenol of Johnson & Johnson.

Datril prepared a direct attack on Tylenol by producing a chemically equivalent product at a lower price. Johnson & Johnson was alerted to the threat by a regional test marketing that Datril conducted prior to going national in the USA.

Johnson & Johnson did nothing. Bristol-Myers prepared a national advertising campaign for Datril with the slogan: 'chemically equivalent to Tylenol but 10% cheaper'. Datril prepared its sales force, stocked the product, and chose launch day.

What did Johnson & Johnson do? Apparently nothing. But on the eve of launch day it sent a credit note to all its retailers for 10 percent of Tylenol's value, and instructed them to reduce the price of the product to consumers accordingly.

The shock for Datril was immense. The staff were taken by surprise. Datril's entire *raison d'être* – price – no longer existed, so there was no value for the retailers or consumers in choosing it. Why change from Tylenol, which was a trusted product, to a newcomer that claimed to be its equal? Datril also lost money in an expensive advertising campaign, which there was now no point in airing. And they had wasted money in sales force training and merchandizing.

And there was no cost to Johnson & Johnson, because all they needed to do was issue some credit notes at the last moment. Datril was dead in the water because Johnson & Johnson waited until the very last moment and the competitor had no hint of its plans. This shows the importance of proper timing management in business – of surprising the enemy and carefully choosing the 'when'.

As Maharbal, the commander of the cavalry said to Hannibal after he won a major victory over the Romans at Cannae: 'Let me now ride towards Rome, as fast as I can, and the Romans will know I have arrived, before being aware I was on the way.'

The 'when' is the third element of competition (along with 'where' and 'how') and will be analyzed in Chapter 5.

2.6 Conclusion

We can be stronger than the enemy. But if we do not know him better than he knows us, if we stretch our forces and resources too thinly, if we do not choose the terrain well, and if we are taken by surprise, what is left in our favor? Not much. If we are not in control of the *how*, *where* and *when* of our fight, we are condemned to defeat.

This is demonstrated by the standing instructions each leader gave their respective armies. King kaMpande told his men not to attack defended positions, 'but catch the British in the open' and Chelmsford instructed that all camps should be 'laagered in the Boer fashion or entrenched'.

The British did not lose again to the Zulus. They had learned their lessons. The war ended with the Zulu king captured and sent into exile. Zululand collapsed into civil war and was never fully independent again.

Figure 2.6 shows the importance of competitor intelligence, focus, careful choice of terrain, and surprise in winning a battle.

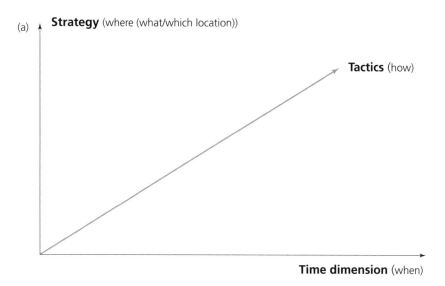

(a)

Strategy (where (what/which location))

Tactics (how)

Time dimension (when)

The impact of Isandlwana lessons on the elements of competition

(b)

Implications	Strategy	Tactics	Time dimension
Four lessons from Isandlwana and Rorke's Drift	Where (what/which location)	How	When
Competitor intelligence 1 Plans (objectives) 2 Characteristics (strengths and weaknesses)	✓	✓	✓
Focus	✓	✓	
Choice of terrain	✓		
Element of surprise			✓
Relevant chapter numbers	3 and 4		5

Figure 2.6 ◆ **The three elements of competition**

Competitor intelligence can inform us about the opponent's characteristics (strengths and weaknesses) and its plans. Competitor intelligence helps with the what, how and when.

Focus is a key determinant in both strategy (where) and tactics (how).

Concentrating on a single decisive moment is fundamental to winning – both before engaging the competitor as well as after, when you concentrate on the opponent's vulnerabilities. The first is strategy, the second is tactics.

Choice of terrain is important for the 'where'. Finally, the element of surprise is relevant to the 'when'.

3

Attack: the six strategic movements

"To defend yesterday is a larger risk than to create tomorrow."

Peter F. Drucker

"Who dares wins."

Motto of British Special Air Service (SAS) Regiment

3.1 Introduction

IN THIS CHAPTER we shall see that there are six possible ways to attack an opponent.

1 Guerrilla.

2 Bypass.

3 Flanking.

4 Frontal attack.

5 Undifferentiated circle.

6 Differentiated circle.

What do we mean by attack? Essentially, we mean going into something *new*:

◆ A new industry in the same geographical area.

◆ The same industry in a new geographical area.

◆ A new industry and a new geographical area.

Additionally, if we enter a new *segment* of the same industry and geographical area on our own initiative, it is an attack. But we enter this segment as a reaction to a competitor, it must be considered as a defensive move. Figure 3.1 summarizes this.

Attack happens if two things happen simultaneously:

1 There is a movement on our part: new geographical area, new industry, and/or a new segment within the same industry and geographical area.

2 This movement occurs on our own initiative for profits or synergy.

Attack = (1) entry + (2) unprovoked

Figure 3.1 summarizes the difference between an attack and a defense.

The difference between the six types of attack listed above is as follows. The first four types of attack concern entry into a *single* segment (whether that segment is the same industry/geographical area or not). The last two (differentiated and undifferentiated circles) refer to entry into *two or more* segments.

To distinguish between the first four types we will consider a simple example – the pizza restaurant business. We will analyze more complex situations later on.

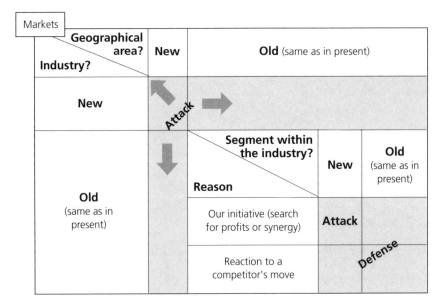

Figure 3.1 ◆ The concept of attack

There are essentially four segments in the pizza service industry:

◆ High quality/service restaurants with an excellent menu and extensive wine list.

◆ Sit-ins with enhanced price and speed of service.

◆ Takeaways.

◆ Home deliveries.

Figure 3.2 illustrates how Pizza Hut fits into these four segments.

Suppose we decide to open a pizza restaurant in our neighborhood. Although there are several firms in this business (Little Caesars, Domino's, Telepizza, Poker's Pizza), we should first concentrate on the industry leader. Why? Because it has the financial resources to try to block our entry (by cutting prices, increasing advertising, etc.). It usually has the best image, visibility, distribution network, and supplier relations.

In this industry, however, the leader (Pizza Hut) does not relate equally to all segments. It is only present in low price sit-ins and takeaways. (Some Pizza Hut restaurants do deliveries. Let us assume that in our neighborhood it does not. We will relinquish this assumption later on.) We will assume that in our

Sit-ins			
High quality and service (good menu, extensive wine list and high price)	Low price and fast service	Takeaways	Home delivery
0%	80%	20%	0%

Pizza Hut turnover in each segment

Figure 3.2 ◆ Pizza Hut market positioning in first neighborhood

neighborhood low price and fast sit-ins represent 80 percent of its sales, and takeaways only 20 percent.

Given the leader's market position we have four ways to enter the pizza business:

◆ If we open a sit-in restaurant with low prices and fast service it will be a frontal attack, because:
   ◆ Pizza Hut is in this segment already,
   ◆ it is important because it represents 80 percent of its turnover.

◆ If we open a small restaurant with a counter and specialize in takeaways, it will be a flanking attack, because:
   ◆ we are entering a segment the leader is currently in, but
   ◆ the leader is not in the segment in strength (represents only 20 percent of its turnover).

◆ If we open a high-quality restaurant it will be a bypass attack, because:
   ◆ Pizza Hut is not in that segment, but
   ◆ we occasionally may steal some customers.

◆ Finally, let's suppose that our restaurant specializes in home deliveries. We effectively operate from a home kitchen answering the phone. This is a guerrilla attack, because:
   ◆ Pizza Hut is not in the segment
   ◆ we are not stealing any customers.

No customers will be stolen because people tend to decide if they want to stay in or go out; once that decision has been made, the choice of provider comes next. Our home delivery client would not go to Pizza Hut on the evening he or she comes to us, even if we did not exist.

What about if we entered two segments at the same time? For example if we offer both takeaway and home deliveries? This would be an undifferentiated circle attack. The two segments benefit from synergy – in both cases there are no tables or waiters.

If we opened a high-price restaurant, with a side counter for takeaways, our strategy would be a differentiated circle:

◆ Circle, because we enter the market through two segments.

◆ Differentiated, since the two segments are very different from each other.

Now let us suppose that Pizza Hut also offers home deliveries in our neighborhood. In this case, Pizza Hut is present in three segments (see Figure 3.3):

◆ Low-price sit-ins (70 percent of turnover).

◆ Takeaways (18 percent of turnover).

◆ Home deliveries (12 percent of turnover).

Here, our entry into the first segment would be a frontal attack (Pizza Hut is present and strong). In either of the other two segments our entry would be a flanking movement (Pizza Hut is present but weak).

A high-price restaurant would be a bypass attack since Pizza Hut is not present but nevertheless we will steal some customers from Pizza Hut sit-ins.

Non-pizza			Pizza				
Low price			Sit-ins				
Other	Ethnic (Indian, Near East, etc.)	Luxury (Top quality and service)	High quality and service (good menu, extensive wine list and high price)	Low price and fast service	Takeaways	Home delivery
				70%	18% Pizza Hut	12%
Bypass	Bypass	Guerrilla	Bypass	Frontal attack	Flanking movement	Flanking movement

Our new restaurant

Figure 3.3 ◆ Pizza Hut marketing positioning in second neighborhood

There is no guerrilla segment here. If we wanted to create one, we would need to open a top-quality, non-pizza restaurant, because that is the only scenario where there would be no crossover between our customers and Pizza Hut's. The restaurants would be very different *both* in terms of type of food and price (a lower-priced, non-pizza restaurant would be a bypass attack).

There are six main aspects to note here. First, industry analysis must be done for each region, one geographical area at a time. This is because the segments where the competitor is present can differ from region to region. And some geographical areas may have specific segments that others do not.

For instance, in financial services, 'emigrants' is an important segment in areas like Mexico and some parts of Central America, since money sent home by emigrants represents a significant percentage of total bank deposits. But in countries where lots of people migrate to instead of from (e.g. USA, Canada) emigrants as a segment are not relevant.

Second, the more complete a segmentation matrix is, the higher the chances of finding a guerrilla segment. A guerrilla segment makes it easier to enter a given market. In our first neighborhood example (Figure 3.2) such a segment exists – home delivery. But in Figure 3.3, we had to further segment the restaurant industry and start a non-pizza luxury restaurant in order to find a guerrilla.

Third, choosing guerrilla, bypass, flanking, or frontal attack depends on the competitor we have in mind. Since each competitor has its own strategy, entry into one segment will represent a frontal attack if the competitor has lots of sales there, but a flanking attack for those for whom it is a marginal segment.

Fourth, it is very important to use the market leader as our reference point to choose the type of attack. The market leader has specific know-how of suppliers, technology, clients, etc. And the market leader benefits most from scale economies, the learning curve, and experience economies. It has a better image and visibility. As it is the most powerful, the leader is the one we should care most about. Even if, because of our overall sales outside the industry, we are larger than a given firm whose sales are greater than ours within the industry, then we must consider ourselves smaller for strategic purposes.

Fifth, imagine a Venn diagram with segment B overlapping segments A and C. B will have a lot in common with both A and C, so attacks by B on either of these two segments would be bypass attacks. But A will have nothing in common with C – so attacks between them would be guerrilla attacks.

Consider an example from the car industry. There is crossover between compacts and subcompacts (very small cars). So attacks by one on the other

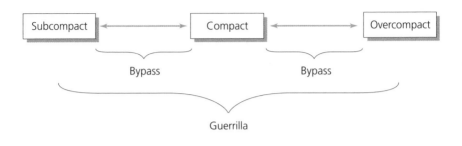

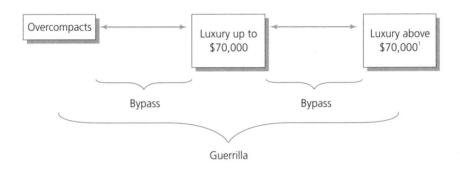

would be bypasses. As would attacks by compacts on 'overcompacts' or super-compacts (small cars, augmented with characteristics of larger cars).

But subcompacts versus overcompacts are guerrilla attacks, because one is not a near-substitute for the other, i.e. usually, two bypasses make one guerrilla.

Finally, competitive success depends on which strategies we follow regarding the dominant industry firm. But it is also contingent upon *how* we implement each strategy. We will look at the 'how' next. Figure 3.4 identifies the differences between the six types of attack.

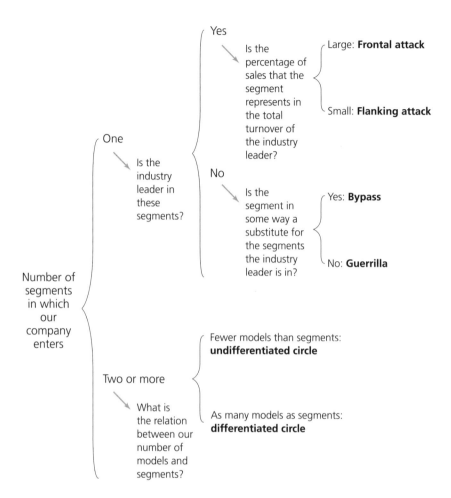

Figure 3.4 ◆ The differences between the six types of attack

3.2 Guerrilla strategy

The enemy advances, we retreat.
The enemy encamps, we harass.
The enemy retreats, we pursue.

Mao Tse-tung

Guerrilla strategies have been followed throughout history by those weaker
than the opponent they fought. The Seminole Indians used them against the

US army in the first half of the eighteenth century; Tito against the Germans in Yugoslavia during World War II; and the Vietcong against the US army in Indochina. All with great success. The stronger lost or had to resort to plots in order to overcome the guerrillas. The Seminole Indians fought a US army four times its size for seven years until they achieved a treaty conceding large territorial possessions. Tito drove the Germans from Yugoslavia. The US army withdrew from Vietnam. And so on.

In business, guerrilla strategies can be used when the largest firms of the industry (use three as a rule of thumb) are not in the segment, and there is very low substitutability between the segment where the largest firms are present, and where they are not.

3.2.1 Types of guerrilla attack

Guerrillas can be one of four main types:

◆ Product[2] guerrillas

◆ Client guerrillas

◆ Need guerrillas

◆ Location guerrillas (different geographical location; distribution channels within a given geographic location; and time)

An example of a product guerrilla is Rent-a-Wreck versus Avis and Hertz. Rent-a-Wreck rents out very old cars at bargain prices. (This is not a substitute. If it was the segment would be a bypass, not a guerrilla.) At the other end of the market, Rolls Royce is a guerrilla against most other types of car. The Jeep is also a guerrilla.

Computer Vision is a product guerrilla against competitors in the software industry, designing systems and programs for three specialist areas: architecture, engineering, and advertising.

A client guerrilla is *Inc.*, which specializes in small business, as opposed to *Fortune*, *Forbes* and *Business Week*.

Examples of need guerrillas are Sorels, which manufacture boots for snow and cold or Kangaroos, which specialize in jogging shoes.

Finally, you can have location guerrillas. For example, Crain's *Chicago Business* attacks *Business Week* and *Fortune* by focussing solely on business in Chicago.

There are four important aspects to consider about guerrillas. First, there are many opportunities in any industry. For example, Kraft is the leader in

cheese production. But in the USA alone there are over 600 cheese companies. Due to the trend towards market fragmentation, (a sub-product of the
overall process of globalization), it's becoming easier all the time to find guerrilla segments in any industry.

For example, Marriott Hotels once concentrated exclusively on first-class
hotels, targeting businessmen. Today, these hotels are still the main business,
but the Marriott Corporation also concentrates on other market segments:
Suites Marriott, Residence Inns Marriott, and Fairfield Inns.

Timex changed from mass to niche marketing. The line Watercolors targets teenagers; BBB (big, bold and beautiful) focusses on women; Carriage
serves men; Victory is for sailors; Velo-trek is for cyclists; and so on.

Second, guerrilla segments *do not have to be non-attractive*. Together with
low market end guerrillas (the cheapest industry brands and models), in any
industry there is a high end. If the largest firms are not there, those segments
can be guerrillas. For example, Steinway in pianos, Piaget ('Why you should
invest in Piaget, the most expensive worldwide watch'), Patek Philipe ('You
really never own a Patek Philipe, you merely take care of it for the next generation'), Chivas Regal ('The world's most expensive whisky'), Rolls Royce,
Bentley, etc.

Third, if a guerrilla strategy does not condemn a company to unattractive
segments, neither does it prevent a firm from *growing*. The secret here is to reinforce one type of guerrilla (e.g. product or client) with another (need, location,
etc.). A good example here is Atral Cipan, a successful pharmaceutical company
with headquarters in Portugal, one of the poorest European countries.

In an industry dominated by giants such as Glaxo and where concentration is ever increasing, Atral Cipan has managed not only to survive through
the last 20 years but also to be extremely profitable. It achieves this by following a double (and thus reinforced) guerrilla strategy, in terms of products
and geographic areas. Sebastião Alves, Atral Cipan's CEO, says 'As the larger
firms grow, they lose interest in market niches and concentrate in larger volume products. Then we jump in.'

This product guerrilla strategy is followed in some of the world's largest
markets such as the European Union, the Far East and Iran. It is then reinforced by a strong presence in geographic markets such as Peru, Colombia,
and Bolivia, and in smaller Central American countries like Costa Rica, where
a weak presence of world industry leaders allows Atral Cipan to be present in
new areas as well as its traditional guerrilla segments, thus reinforcing its
geographical presence.

Atral Cipan keeps away from the large markets favored by worldwide leaders – Mexico, Brazil and Argentina. This reinforcement of product guerrilla
tactics by geographical guerrilla tactics allows Atral Cipan growth and
increased profits without having to confront the industry's major players. It's
important in pharmaceuticals because large companies benefit from high-scale
economies in product development and marketing.

It's worth remembering that many of today's multinationals started out as
guerrilla players. Many Japanese companies, for example, used guerrilla tactics extensively to conquer international markets.

In computers, electronics and transport, Japanese companies introduced
low-price, smaller versions of products on American soil that rivalled home-
grown brands. Names such as Honda, Suzuki, Yamaha, and Kawasaki introduced motorbikes with much less power at a fraction of the price of a Harley
Davidson. For many years Sony TVs were much less expensive than rival
American brands – they were smaller and more compact, but this became perceived as a benefit rather than an inferior attribute.

3.2.2 How to implement a guerrilla strategy

There are nine simple steps to follow. The first is indicated in Figure 3.5. This
shows the strategic square that shapes every firm's activity. Any company must
have a product or service that satisfies a given requirement of a certain type of
client, in a given location.

A large corporation will have many strategic squares by enlarging one or
more of the four sides, depending upon where it envisages the greater opportunities and/or synergy.

Gerber, for instance, has a basic strategic square that sells baby walkers to
US markets. Its extended strategic square includes children's clothes, high
chairs, baby lotions, and even life insurance for parents.

Regardless of how many strategic squares a firm has, the way to be a guerrilla is to look at all four sides of the square and see if you can think of a type
of product, client, need or location in which the three largest players are not
present and where there is no cross-over between products.

Remember that a guerrilla can exist either because it is 'different'[3] or
because it is 'complementary'. An example of the former is the subcompact
car – intrinsically different from a station wagon, a wagon or an overcompact.
The guerrilla player is different. But the client who buys *Business Week* and
lives in Chicago may also buy Crain's *Chicago Business*. The guerrilla is

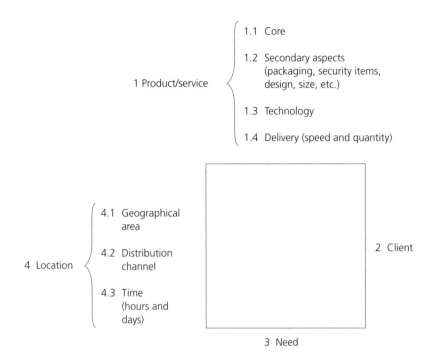

Figure 3.5 ◆ The strategic square – the first step in building a guerrilla strategy

complementary. The small entrepreneur, who has a subscription to *Forbes*, may also be a regular of *Inc*. Many guerrillas are complementary: Sorels boots complement standard footwear. Chivas Regal can be a whisky for special occasions to replace lower-priced brands. The sporty Tag Heuer brand is a watch to wear only on special occasions, but that doesn't mean you won't have a cheaper watch. So when checking the four sides of the strategic square in Figure 3.5, search not only for alternatives but complements. That way you can create a much larger number of guerrillas.

Next, one must distinguish between guerrillas that are attacking three large firms in an industry, attacking two or just attacking the biggest. [4]

The next step is to evaluate each segment in terms of:

◆ Capacity. Can we do it well? Do we have the required skills? [5]

◆ Fit. Is the segment synergistic with those we are presently in?

◆ Growth. How attractive is the guerrilla segment in terms of margin by unit sales and sales volume?

The higher a segment rates in each of these quality characteristics, the better it is.

The best way to find attractive guerrillas is to look for economical, political and social trends that the industry leader has not taken advantage of, and find out where we can be competitive.

Social trends can be based on health or lifestyles. Health trends have led to the success of light and non-alcoholic beers and caffeine-free and diet colas. Social pressure against obesity led McDonald's to introduce a variety of foods marketed as low fat.

Lifestyle trends can be powerful, too. An example is the 'quick casual' restaurants typified by Panera Bread and Cosi in the USA and Pret A Manger in the UK. Prices are higher than in the burger bars, but the meals are very different. A Panera turkey panini includes smoked turkey, spinach and artichoke spread, caramelized onions and tomato, and parmesan cheese, all grilled on basil pesto focaccia bread.

Besides profiting from environmental trends, one must satisfy them as well – to achieve customer satisfaction and brand loyalty. Take Vlasic foods, a giant in the preserved foods market. In the early 1980s it tried to push a small pickles company called Farmen's out of the pickles market. Vlasic decreased its pickles price from $1.89 to 79 cents and doubled its advertising budget.

Farmen's decided not to enter a price war. They maintained their prices and relied on the image and quality of their products and the loyalty of their distribution outlets. The result? Three years later Farmen's market share outnumbered that of Vlasic by a ratio of ten to one. And Farmen's sales had also increased since the Vlasic advertising campaign had the effect of increasing the demand for pickles as a food category, which primarily benefited Farmen's and not Vlasic.

The fifth way to be a good guerrilla is to keep the numbers down and have small unit sales. Large firms do not like small segments since they demand more of their time than they feel their small size deserves. This is why French public works giant Grand Travaux de Marseille pulled out of working in small European countries such as Greece and Portugal, despite closer European integration, and despite an initial phase of multi-country presence within Europe. Most large investment bankers behave similarly, imposing a floor of $5 million beneath which they will not analyze any investments – regardless of the sector's growth and profit potential.

Notice that size is measured in terms of unit sales – not sales value. Sales value is obtained by multiplying unit sales by unit margin. Even if the unit margin is high, the effect of repulsing large firms continues. American Motors' Jeep was a guerrilla that the industry giants did not bother to attack, not because its unit margin was low (it was not), but because, from the start, the segment seemed relatively small. Yearly unit sales were little over 10,000 a year in the first few years.

Lack of opposition for 11 years (until Ford launched the Pickup F250 in 1959), enabled American Motors to grow Jeep sales. In spite of new Ford and GM models, Jeep sales reached nearly half a million in the late 1990s.

American Motors did not achieve this success in other segments where it operated; on the contrary, it lost money in all of them.

It can even be argued that high unit margins increase the power of a guerrilla, since a high unit margin is more uncertain than sales volume (it depends on intangibles such as image) and usually requires a personalized service that large companies do not have a special vocation for. So it is all to the good if top of unit sales are low and unit margin is high. The larger corporations have insufficient time for the first, and lack of aptitude for the second.

Small numbers mean low unit sales, which can be due to artificial barriers (customs, technical barriers[6]) or natural market barriers, which are often a consequence of different cultural values or tastes in different geographical areas. In such cases, globalization is restricted and large firms cannot envisage a unique, single product/model to be sold worldwide.

But a segment can be large and still be the habitat for small firms, for one or more of the following reasons:

1 Scale economies are low, because:

    1.1 cost reductions are not significant (whatever the level of production); and/or

    1.2 cost decreases stop at very low quantities of output; and/or

    1.3 technology is not of mass, standardized production, but of unit or small batch.

Segments in cutlery, high fashion, valves for nuclear plants, bearings for military aircraft, and gas and air compressors of over 1000 horsepower fall into these areas.

2 The learning curve effect is also weak (for reasons similar to 1.1 or 1.2).[7] Examples are speciality textiles, specialist magazines, clothes (dresses, handbags), and frozen foods.

3 Intangibles such as quality of service and staff motivation are critical for success. Examples are high fashion and advertising, lingerie, and perfumes. It's easier for smaller firms to achieve high levels of service and motivation.

4 High speed of innovation – large firms tend to be slower than smaller ones, due to increased bureaucracy and rules.

5 The client doesn't want a single supplier offering a wide range of products. It used to be the case in the sanitation industry that a municipality would launch four different public tenders for a waste treatment plant: one for the project; another for the building; another for the equipment; and a fourth for management. Nowadays, the trend is towards one key bid, where each bidder places a tender for the four services together. A large firm will have most if not all of the required specialities. A smaller firm will not. So the smaller firm has to form alliances with other firms to make bids, which are time consuming. Eventually small firms tend to work as subcontractors supplying a given speciality for large firms, which become their clients instead of the final entity.

6 Finally, transportation costs are high (in the construction industry for example). The more this reason becomes relevant, the more supply will be divided among smaller firms, regardless of the segment's size.

The seventh guideline when becoming a guerrilla is to choose a segment where you will be first, if you can. This can either be because it is new or because for one reason or another, no one else has moved into it.

To have the first move advantage is generally a source of strong competitive advantage. You will have a stronger position in the minds of customers. And you have more time to establish links with suppliers and distribution channels.

Any product segment carries dozens if not hundreds of brands. But having been the first to move into an industry segment is frequently an advantage.

Take the imported beer segment in the USA. The first brand imported just after World War II was Heineken. Fifty years later which has the largest share? Heineken, with 30 percent, in spite of there being 425 brands of imported beer in the US market.

The story repeats itself with Coca-Cola, Hertz, IBM, Federal Express, Kleenex, Xerox, Band-aid, Scotch Tape, etc. They all teach the same lesson: being first places you strongly in the customer's mind. We return to this subject when discussing the pre-emptive strike as a form of defense (Chapter 4, section 4.3).

The eighth step to being a successful guerrilla is to lay low and make no waves. Even if your chosen market segment is away from the industry zones where the larger firms feed, and even if your market segment is unnatural for them (for scale economies, geographic fragmentation, etc.), it is not a good idea to keep a high profile.

Advertising your profits, marketing your plans, and publicizing your successes is bad for business. The big companies in the industry will resent your high profile and may decide to enter your segment and compete directly with you to force you to withdraw from the market. The bigger they are, the greater the threat, since they can more easily afford to lose money than you. So, the essence of a guerrilla is to stay away, not only from the larger firms' segments, but also from their minds. Montaigne once said, 'the way of living well is through living discreetly.' In nature, discretion is called camouflage. This implies that the most skilful animals are not necessarily the strongest. As in business, the best strategy is not to be seen.

Give yourself time to grow and then you can act differently – but not until then. We will get back to this topic in Chapter 6, when discussing how firms internationalize.[8]

The final criteria for staging guerrilla warfare is to reinforce one type of guerrilla with another. We looked at Atral Cipan earlier, which reinforced product guerrillas with geographical guerrillas. But even if we stick to one type of guerrilla (say product) the possibilities for growth are susbtantial. Take the case of Medeva, a relatively new British firm when Bernard Taylor joined it from Glaxo in 1980. Taylor saw a chance to build a company by buying drugs and vaccines that larger companies no longer wanted because their sales were too low. (Note again the importance of small numbers as a criteria for a good guerrilla.)

But not just any drugs. Taylor focussed on products that treated a narrow spectrum of ailments, especially bronchial conditions like influenza and asthma. 'By targeting a few clinical areas,' Taylor explains, 'Medeva's salesman can focus on doctors treating those conditions, and usually have more success with those doctors than a salesman promoting a wider range of drugs.'

The result was better sales and pre-tax earnings year after year. 'I saw Medeva as a new way to build a pharmaceutical company,' said Taylor.

Only after we have a solid presence in one segment should we think of entering another.

Figure 3.6 illustrates the nine steps to becoming a guerrilla.

Number	Description	Rationale
I	Use all sides of the strategic square	Guerillas can be product, client, need or location based
II	Search for differentiation and symbiosis	Both originate guerrillas in any of the four sides of the strategic square
III	Select those segments generated in steps I and II that are guerrillas for all three of the largest firms, not just for the largest or second largest	The segment is further away from the industry zone dominated by all three larger firms
IV	Evaluate each guerrilla segment in terms of: 1 Do we have the required skills? 2 Is the segment synergistic with our present operations? 3 Attractiveness (growth, margin and unit sales)	'Quality of the segment' (money-making potential)
V	Small numbers in demand (not low unit margin)	Unnatural habits for large firms
VI	Small numbers in supply	
VII	If possible select a segment where you are first	To gain first move advantage
VIII	Lay low	Calling attention to yourself would give the opposition an advantage
IX	Reinforce one type of guerrilla with another	Enable growth

Figure 3.6 ◆ The nine steps to create a guerrilla

As a final point, note that when entering into a new industry or geographic area, a guerrilla strategy is advisable both for small and large firms. Firms whose total sales or assets (outside the industry or geographic area) are higher, are superior to those of the firm with the largest share within the industry. Guerrilla strategy is not synonymous with small firm strategy. A guerrilla is advisable for everything new – even when the newcomer is big.

Why? Because even if the firm with the largest share within the industry is smaller than the newcomer, the former nevertheless possesses three important advantages:

1 Greater industry know-how (clients, suppliers and technology).

2 Better image (which is frequently specific).

3 Larger scale, experience and synergy economies (which are frequently industry specific, and thus easier to exploit within industries rather than across them).

What matters most is size within the industry, not outside it. Small firms need a sound strategy more than larger ones, since they lack resources to recover from their mistakes. (As with all strategy this applies to businesses, countries or people. A large country recovers more easily from a major defeat than a small one. A wealthy person recovers from a setback more easily than a poor one.)

What if no guerrilla segment is available in terms of the criteria presented in Figure 3.6? Then one should reject all guerrillas and instead opt for the so-called bypass attack.

3.3 Bypass

In World War II, General MacArthur chose not to directly engage the Japanese forces when he began the attack that led ultimately to Japan's surrender. Instead they used a bypass attack. 'American troops attacked and conquered weak areas with minimum losses,' said Japanese General Matsuichi Ino. 'They interrupted our supply lines and, weakened us with hunger. They searched for our weak areas and submerged us.'

In the second Gulf War against Iraq in 2003, the initial strategy of the allies was also to bypass Iraq major cities (Nasiriya, Basra, etc.), avoid major battles, and move directly to Baghdad. That allowed allied forces to travel 300 miles and reach the outskirts of Baghdad in only seven days. An astonishingly short period of time in terms of warfare.

In business, as in war, the essential characteristics of a bypass attack are:

1 Attack is upon a (market) area where competition is *not* present; but

2 Our presence in that area alarms or even disrupts competition (because there is crossover between our products and the opponents').

That was the strategy followed by foreign car manufacturers when entering the US transport vehicle industry. Volkswagen, Toyota, Honda, and Mazda initially offered only subcompact cars, which GM, Ford, and Chrysler resisted offering, for fear of cannibalizing their own sales of larger and more profitable (per unit sold) cars. Henry Ford II used to say that mini cars equalled mini profits.

Cannibalism is a key concept when discussing bypass and will be discussed in full later. We will start by looking at the following:

◆ The four types of bypass.

◆ One type that is specially important.

◆ How to do them.

◆ A few major aspects of bypass.

3.3.1 The four types of bypass

As with guerrillas, there are four types: products, clients, needs and location bypass.

Dec's introduction of minicomputers was a product bypass to IBM (which at that moment was offering only mainframes). Later, Apple performed a bypass on Dec's minis with its microcomputers (and also on IBM's, which after considerable hesitation opted to launch a minicomputer line too).

When Control Data launched the mini supercomputers, a category of machine in-between IBM's mainframes and Cray Computers' supercomputers it was performing a bypass on both firms.

There are many ways of using product characteristics to perform bypass strategies. One is price. BMW series 3 and 5 bypassed Cadillac[9] through higher price and quality. La Quinta is a bypass of Day Inn, which in itself is a bypass of Holiday Inn, since all three are in distinct price classes of the motel business. In any industry each category is a bypass to its nearest rival on the price scale. Look at the diagram opposite, which uses European supermarkets as an example.

Size is another way to bypass. It can be small (Nissan Micra, Tummy TV, or Sharp Pocket calculators) or large (oversize Head tennis rackets, Pepsi 1.5 liter bottle, TV mega screens, or Eurico brand shoes specializing in the large numbers for men and women).

Just as with guerrillas, the other three sides of the strategic square can be used to perform bypasses:

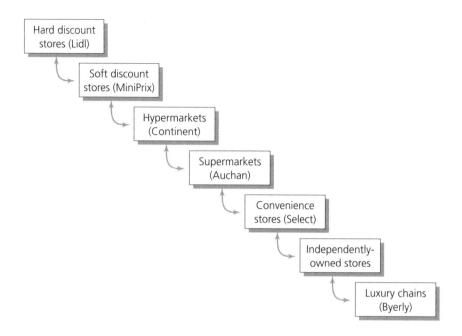

◆ *Need*: in beers, Michelob is for the weekends, Miller for the blue collars, Coors for the Middle West. Lone Star uses the image of Texas, Budweiser Light offers low calories. Bell whisky is an example of flanking based on need; in Europe it is positioned as the ideal brand for cocktails and mixings.

◆ *Client*: enterprise Rent-a-car focusses on the insurance replacement market. This is an area that the airport giants do not pursue. The client is the insurance company.

◆ *Location*: this side of the strategic square is especially important for bypass. French distribution chain Intermarché places its supermarkets outside and around major urban cities, but not within them.

Location can also be in terms of distribution channels. We saw before how home delivery allowed Domino's Pizza to circumvent market leader Pizza Hut's dominance of physical locations. In perfumes Revlon specializes in drugstores, so Avon concentrates on door-to-door and Yves Roche focuses on direct mail. Dell was the first computer company to focus on direct marketing of computers – reducing its real estate costs enabled it to compete on price. Examples can be taken from any industry.

Sara Lee is the world's largest maker of stockings and socks. Much of that fact is due to its brand L'Eggs, a pantyhose brand. Sara Lee looked for a new distribution channel and chose supermarkets. Their research showed that women visit one at least once a week. Sara Lee was the first in that specific location – no competition. Today, L'Eggs is the number one pantyhose brand in the USA with 25 percent market share, accounting for two thirds of Sara Lee's hosiery sales.

It's important though to be aware that performing bypasses on the market leader(s) means taking a risk. Indeed, our segment is similar to some of those where the industry leaders are. Because there is some degree of crossover between the segments, we steal some of their customers. Our success means less turnover and profit for them.

Since the essence of a bypass is contiguity, the consequence is disturbing for a major opponent. So they may try to crush the attack by improving their present offer (lower prices, improved performance, more advertising) or by entering into our bypass segment with a new model to compete head-on with us.

This defense strategy of the market leader is called blocking (see Chapter 4), and is something we wish to avoid at any cost. We need time to grow and consolidate our presence in the segment.

This takes us to the criteria a firm should follow when performing a bypass.

3.3.2 Criteria for bypasses

First, select a market segment whose margin per unit of sales is lower than that of the market leader.

Why? Because if the industry leader decides to block our entry by launching a new model to compete head-on with us, it will be cannibalizing its own sales in its higher margin segments. (And even more so if it decides to lower prices in those segments to fight us in the bypass segment.)

A new lower-priced model will attract some of the present customers from other more profitable segments, thus hurting the leader's sales. Since it may not be clear what the growth prospects of the bypass segment are, or how those prospects will improve with the presence of the market leader (due to its better image), it is likely that the leader will hesitate: should it block, or not? While it hesitates, time goes by, enabling us to strengthen our position near customers, distribution channels, and suppliers. When we are finally attacked, we will have had time to consolidate our position.

The important point here is that *fear of cannibalism reinforces any doubts the leader may have* regarding blocking our entry in a bypass segment. To create this environment our unit margin must be lower than the leaders' segments.

That has been the story of the subcompacts versus GM, Ford and Chrysler; Timex or Seiko versus established Swiss brands; Wilkinson Sword's stainless steel razor blades versus Gillete's carbon steel blades; and so on.

The second important criteria a bypass segment must satisfy is to have an expected growth rate not too far superior to that of the segments the leader(s) is in. If it does, it will erase any hesitation the leader may have in blocking the newcomer's entry.

The third step is to look for segments where, if the leader blocks us, it will weaken its own position.

Figure 3.7 provides an example. Let's suppose that segment 1 is a bypass of segment 2, and segment 6 a bypass of segment 7. Let us also suppose that the segment leaders in both 2 and 7 are different, and that market shares are as shown in Figure 3.7. They are very similar in segment 2, and the leader has a considerable advantage in segment 7.

Which segment should our firm enter into? The answer is segment 1. Why? Because the leader of segment 2 will have extreme difficulty in blocking us. To do so it would need to take resources away from segment 2. It cannot afford to do this since it would compete head-on for market share.

However, the situation in segment 7 is different. Here, the leader has considerable share advantage over competitors. So it can afford to divert resources from this segment to block our entry into segment 7.

The fourth criteria is to select the segment that will offer the greatest synergy to enter other segments later on, i.e. the segment that shares the most resources with our present one and with others in the industry – distribution channels, raw materials suppliers, etc. Look for similarity of machinery, components, parts, installations, and so on.

All other conditions equal, that is the segment we should opt for. It will be easier to defend if it is more synergistic with our present operations, and it will provide us with a foot in the door to enter other segments of the industry, which we can use later on to enter our segment of choice.

There are other criteria similar to those we identified for guerrillas:

◆ Try to be first in the segment.

◆ Search for bypasses using the four sides of the strategic square in Figure 3.5.

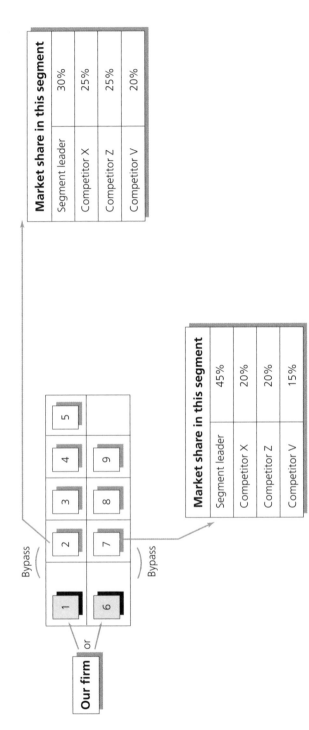

Figure 3.7 ◆ Choosing which segment to bypass

A bypass strategy should be made on segment 1, not 6, because if the industry strategy leader blocks our entry in the former, it will weaken its center.

Number	Description	Rationale
I	Our segment should have lower unit margin than that of the leader's segments	If the industry leader blocks our entry it will cannibalize its sales and profits
II	Similar or inferior growth rates	Enhances leader's hesitation
III	Bypass to segment where the leader's position is weaker	If the leader blocks, it will weaken its center
IV	Greatest synergy	To facilitate both that segment's defense and future entry into others of the industry
V	Be the first	First-move advantage
VI	Try all four sides of the strategic square (in Figure 3.5)	Bypasses can be product, client, need or location based
VII	Give special attention to location (geographical areas, distribution channels and time)	Usually a great source for bypasses
VIII	Select the segment that is a bypass to more rather than fewer leaders	Disturbs fewer industry leaders
IX	Small numbers in supply	Unnatural habitat for large firms
X	Choose best segment in terms of: 1 Do we have the required skills? 2 How attractive is it (in terms of the sales volume growth rate and unit margin)?	Quality of the segment
XI	Lay low	Not calling attention to yourself creates a tactical advantage
XII	Reinforce one bypass with another	Enable growth

Figure 3.8 ◆ Twelve steps to create a bypass

◆ Select the segment that represents a bypass to all or most of the three leaders (otherwise the segment is a flanking or a frontal attack, both of which are harder to win).

◆ Choose bypasses characterized by small numbers in supply.

◆ Choose the segment with the highest quality (meaning that we have the required strengths, and that the segment has strong financial potential).

◆ Keep one's head down.

◆ Reinforce success with success.

The latter means two things. First, concentrate on total dominance of the segment. Go after market share. When that is achieved, reinforce bypasses only with further bypasses (or better still with guerrillas). Avoid performing flanking or frontal attacks.

The guerrilla criteria of small numbers in demand does not apply here, since we have opted for a segment that already has low unit margin and a growth rate not far too superior to the industry leader's segments. Figure 3.8 summarizes these criteria.

3.3.3 More thoughts on bypasses

As with guerrillas, bypasses do not have to be low margin segments. Examples are Byerly's high-quality supermarket, Reidenbacker ('the world's most expensive popcorn'); Häagen-Dazs ('the top quality ice cream'), and Michelob ('one should drink something special at the weekend'). Levi's, Lee and Wrangler are the market leaders in jeans, but Murjani, Calvin Klein, Jordache and Sassoon do very well by focussing on the upper end of the market – 'designer' jeans.

Regarding unit margin, however, there is a great difference between guerrillas and bypasses. Guerrilla segments could be of high unit margin and not tempt the industry leaders to enter as long as they were low sales volume. But bypasses must be of lower unit margin than that of the leader's segments, otherwise the risk of the leader blocking our entry is high.

Bypasses are such powerful strategies that today the marketplace is full of examples of firms that are set up, enter a segment, and dominate without ever confronting the leader head-on.

The US bicycle industry was once dominated by Schwinn, with 25 percent of the market. Then in 1974 Gary Fisher built the first off-road bike with a wide gear range and heavy-duty braking. He named his creation the mountain bike. After that, Schwinn was never the same again.

A wide range of mountain bike manufacturers rode into the market: Trek pioneered carbon-fiber frames; Cannondale used aluminium-frame bikes; and Specialized Bicycle Components concentrated on mountain-bike racing. By 1992, two-thirds of adult bikes sold were mountain bikes. And Schwinn? It was bankrupt.

Now under new management, Schwinn is trying to pedal its way back into the bicycle business. With mountain bikes, naturally.

So bypasses are powerful. But they are riskier than guerrillas since they steal customers away from the leaders. The risk of provoking a reaction on the part of the leader is nothing though, compared to a flanking movement – which we turn to next.

3.4 Flanking attack

A flanking movement is a third type of attack. However, it is more difficult to achieve successfully than either a guerrilla or a bypass, since here our firm enters a segment containing one of the industry leaders (albeit not in strength).

A flanking attack is one against a segment that is of less importance to the leader – say below 15 percent of its turnover. Above that figure and the attack would be classed as frontal.

General MacArthur provided a military example of the flanking movement during the Korean War in the 1950s. After North Korea invaded South Korea, the South Koreans were cut off at the bottom of the peninsula and about to surrender to the surrounding invaders. MacArthur did not land his troops in the South Korean stronghold as everybody expected. Instead, he landed further north at Inchon, in the middle of the Korean peninsula – away from the battlefront – where the North Korean army was present, but not in strength. This move divided the peninsula in two and effectively isolated the majority of the North Korean army from its supply sources.

In business, a flanking attack also has these characteristics. You engage the enemy but not where it is strong.

Most regional banks make flanking movements against national banks. Chemical, Citibank and Bank of America are flanked by United Jersey Bank in New Jersey, Long Island Trust in Long Island, Fidelity National Bank in Georgia, California Thrift Savings & Loan in California, and so on.

Or consider the flanking attacks of Japanese car companies when they entered Europe. In the early 1960s they entered Finland and Switzerland.

Later in the 1960s they entered Holland, Belgium and Luxemburg. Norway and Sweden were attacked next in the early 1970s. By the mid-1970s they had reached the UK. France and Germany were left until the late 1970s and Italy was only infiltrated in the early 1980s.

In each case, the strength of the national car industry in each country at the time was considered as the first criteria. It was highest in Germany, and minimal in Finland and Switzerland.

Besides *geographical flanking*, three other types of flanking can occur: *product*, *need*, and *client*.

Examples of *product flanking* are provided by Porche, Maserati, and Lamborghini against car leaders – Toyota, General Motors, Ford, etc.

Most of Pizza Hut's sales come from low price, sit-down restaurants. Takeaways account for only one quarter of the turnover. So firms like Little Caesars and Poker's Pizza that specialize in takeaways are performing *need flanking* movements on Pizza Hut. Emery Air Freight, which specializes in mid- to heavyweight delivery of packages, performs need flanking on DHL and Federal Express.

Finally, flanking can also be based on *clients*. BMW aims for a higher social class. Wendy's aims for older customers, SAS Airlines targets executives, and Pepsi tries to gain a younger audience than Coca-Cola.

Whatever its geographic, product, need or client, flanking movements are much more difficult to perform successfully than the guerrillas and bypasses.

Due to the increased risk of retaliation in making flanking movements, there are five criteria that must be observed.

3.4.1 Criteria

Never weaken the center. Only when one controls a given segment, in terms of market share, should one move into a new one. Otherwise your ambition risks being greater than your capacity.

You need to be prepared for retaliation. That requires building up resources for the struggle, without weakening your capacity to fight for share in your older segments.

Sears Roebuck over-extended its resources in this way and became a prey of specialists, at both ends of the market.

Surprise is the second criteria for success in flanking. Entry into a new market segment without warning prevents competitors having time to prepare or react to a new advertising campaign or an improved list of products. They will become confused if taken by surprise, which leads to them becoming demoralized.

If surprise is not possible, then at least perform the flanking attack with great speed. Speed can act as a substitute for surprise. Iglo, Unilever's frozen food brand, which dominates Europe, provides a good example. Nestlé decided to use its brand Findus to attack in a few countries of least value to Unilever: Spain, Italy, Greece, and Portugal.

But Nestlé did this so slowly that every one of its actions was matched and even surpassed by Unilever. When Nestlé offered improved food containers to retailers, so did Unilever. When Nestlé cut prices, or increased variety, Unilever responded. Instead of doing everything at once to overcome Unilever, Nestlé did it sequentially and at a pace that Unilever was able to match.

The third rule of a flanking attack is that it must be performed in the segment where the *competition's commitment is lower*. If the commitment is lower, so is the willingness to devote resources to retaliation.

There are four reasons for this. First, one segment can be less relevant than another in terms of the percentage of sales it represents for the competitor. Second, strong retribution is less likely if the segment we enter is less synergistic with other segments the competitor is in.

For image and emotional reasons, companies are more likely to defend segments if they were the first to market in it or if the product has become synonymous with their brand.

Fourth, consider the *Boston Consulting Group* matrix, which distinguishes four types of business unit: stars, cash cows, question marks, and dogs.[10] The first is more likely to be defended than the second, the second more than the third, and the third more than the last (see Figure 3.9).

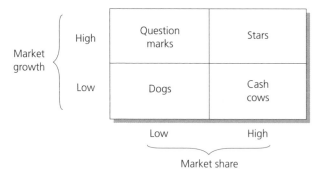

Figure 3.9 ◆ The Boston Consulting Group matrix

Number	Description		Rationale
I	Do not weaken the center		Since flanking requires high resources for a market share fight, it is important that the required resources be taken away from other segments without creating the risk of eroding our position there
II	Surprise		Confuses and demoralizes the competitor, making it less likely to react in time and with quality
III	Speed (act at a fast pace)		Reinforces the effect of surprise, making it difficult for the competitor to react in time
IV	Enter a segment where the competitor's commitment is lower	4.1 Low sales percentage	The competitor has less to lose
		4.2 Not a core (in synergy terms) segment for the competitor	What is at stake for the competitor is only the value of the attacked segment
		4.3 Not one of the segments where the competitor originally entered	There are no image or emotional reasons for the competitor to retaliate
		4.4 Preferably attack a dog or a question mark, rather than a cash cow or a star	The former are less important SBUs for the competitor
V	Choose the best segment in terms of: 1 attractiveness; 2 our strengths matching the segment success factors; and 3 synergy with our other segments		Quality of the segment

Figure 3.10 ◆ Criteria for a sound flanking attack

Stars are the future of the company since these are the business units in high-growth markets. Cash cows are important because, although in low-growth markets, they provide most of the company cash.

Question marks, however, are problems a competitor may be happy to get rid of, or are at least of dubious value to fight for. Indeed, our flanking attack may provide the competitor's management with the pretext it needs to drop it. Dogs are likely to be dropped if they are attacked.

Attack dogs first, then question marks, then cash cows.

Finally, the segment should naturally be:

◆ *Attractive* in terms of growth prospects, unit margin and volume of sales.

◆ High in *success factors that match our strengths*, and

◆ Preferably *synergistic* with our other segments.

Unless these five criteria are closely followed, a flanking movement risks failure. The benefit of experience is with the competitor and you are forcing it. Figure 3.10 illustrates this.

3.5 Frontal attacks

A frontal attack means two things. First, you enter into a competitor's segment and, second, that segment is very relevant for that competitor in terms of sales, i.e. the segment represents a large share of the competitor's total turnover.

Therefore frontal attacks are serious engagements, because you are attacking a competitor where it is strong.

It is difficult to succeed with this strategic movement because one forces the competitor to retaliate strongly unless it accepts losing lots of sales. However, as the competitor has a high percentage of its sales in the segment, it is unlikely to do so. And this almost inevitable retaliation is likely to be successful – as the competitor knows the terrain so well. Figure 3.11 illustrates why our chances of success are so slim.

This is why, in military history, so many frontal attacks have failed despite the attacker having superiority in numbers. Seventy thousand Romans failed to defeat 50,000 Carthaginians at Cannae. Sixty-seven thousand English held their ground against 74,000 French soldiers at Waterloo. At Balaclava, in the famous English Charge of the Light Brigade, 500 of the 673 cavalry men died. True, there have been frontal attack successes: Bunker Hill in the US War of Independence, the French against a coalition of several countries at

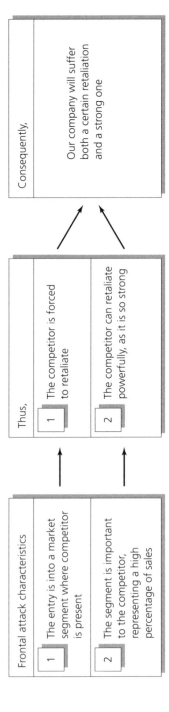

Figure 3.11 ◆ Why most frontal attacks fail

Austerlitz, and El Alamein in World War II. But most frontal attacks end in failure.

Boots using its 'Rufen' brand to attack Upjohn's 'Motrin' brand is an example of a failed frontal attack in business, as is the *International Herald Tribune*'s attempt to dislodge *The Times*' position as a morning newspaper. Another example is Procter & Gamble's failed attempt to use Tide against Unilever's Omo in the UK.

Just as in war, one can find a few instances of successful business frontal attacks: Playtex against Tampax in the 1970s, Procter & Gamble and Jergens against Minnetonka's liquid soap in the 1980s, and Fresh Express against Dole Food Co. in the 1990s. But they are the exception.

3.5.1 Using frontal attacks

Frontal attacks must be performed with the utmost care and closely obey the following eight rules.

First, frontal attacks should be conducted on narrow fronts. That means in one market segment only.

Frontal attacks are difficult enough without spreading your forces too thinly. Al Ries and Jack Trout point out that this frequently happens:[11] 'Would a general attack simultaneously in several points at the same time? Never. Would a manager attack in various segments at the same time? Yes. They do it all the time'.

Take Pepsi. It was for a long time engaged in three simultaneous head-on battles. The first was with Coca-Cola in soft drinks. Then Pepsi bought itself another major battle by entering the snack food market, through acquiring Frito-Lay. Finally, Pepsi involved Pizza Hut, Taco Bell, and Kentucky Fried Chicken, all of which it owned, in a major battle with McDonald's, Burger King, and several pizza companies.

The result was that, in spite of being larger than each of its three major opponents (Procter & Gamble and Mars in snacks, McDonald's in fast food, and Coca-Cola in soft drinks), Pepsi did considerably worse than any of these three in terms of results.

Of course, there were positive synergies among the three main Pepsi businesses: the fast food outlets sold Frito-Lay snacks and Pepsi beverages. But there were also negative effects. For example, other chains and independent restaurants preferred to buy Coca-Cola rather than Pepsi because they viewed it as a competitor.

Had Pepsi decided to concentrate its forces in one or at most two market segments, its chances of success in each of them would have been greater, as it would have been easier to dominate the focussed segments, increase its market share in them, and harvest the benefits.

Pepsico later confirmed the soundness of these arguments. It sold its $14 billion restaurant business (Taco Bell, Kentucky Fried Chicken, and Pizza Hut) and the group was re-christened Tricon Global Restaurants. Since the sale, both Pepsi and Tricon have done very well.

Another example is Philips. It is engaged in major battles with Intel in the chip business, with Sega and Nintendo in the video game business, against General Electric in the lighting business, against Sony in the video and camcorder business, and against many players in the cable television, video rental, and computer industries. Consequently, during the past decade, Philips stock has been an underperformer – it nearly collapsed in 1990 with a loss of $2.3 billion.

The lesson is that however big you are, you are not big enough to have several fights on your hands at the same time. Even if you hold your ground, or do well, you could do considerably better if you take on one competitor at a time.

This focus is the basis of success for many companies. As von Clausewitz, the great interpreter of Napoleon, put it, 'an army should not be in a feeble way in several places – but in strength in a few places'. If we divide, we weaken. If we concentrate, we strengthen.

From the need to focus follows a second major principle to follow on frontal attacks. Besides focussing on one segment, one should also take on one competitor (in that segment) at a time. This reinforces focus: one segment and, within it, one competitor.

Otherwise what? Disaster. Take Royal Crown. In the early 1970s, it went through several major changes. It restructured its franchise system, hired a veteran from Coca-Cola and Pepsi, engaged in a major advertising campaign, and then, in a statement from the head of Crown's advertising agency, announced publicly: 'we are after the jugular vein'. Not of Coca-Cola or of Pepsi – but of both. Royal Crown's market share went down from 6 percent to 2 percent.

So the first principle is focus. There is an Arab proverb that says, 'I against my brother; I and my brother against my cousin; I, my brother and my cousin against my family; I and my whole family against my neighbor; I, my family and my neighbor against my town; I and my town against the world.'

The third rule when attacking frontally is to strike at the competitor's *weakest point*. Everyone has strengths and weaknesses. A good example is provided by Campbell's Soup when it decided to enter the TV dinner market. It looked at the leader (Swanson) and asked itself: What are the weak points in its products? What are the characteristics that clients complain about? Through market research it found that customers wanted a diet product, which had less salt, and a more attractive, informative package. Consequently, Campbell's Soup launched a product that fitted these requirements. Sales boomed as the health-conscious market grew.

In the early 1960s Toyota performed marketing research on Volkswagen (VW) Beetle customers to discover what they disliked about the car. Not enough legroom, no armrests, a rough drive, and high fuel consumption were the issues. Toyota focussed on improving its subcompact Corona model to meet these requirements before entering the US market.

To look for the weak spot means to strike in the right place, rather than to strike many times. However, when looking for the 'Achilles' heel' there are three main things that must be kept in mind.

First, *how to find it*. Sometimes the sources are the customers, as the above examples of Swanson and the VW Beetle illustrate. Sometimes the competitor's weak spot is suggested by social trends: diet soft drinks; caffeine-free soft drinks; light beers. On other occasions, culture provides an opportunity, as in the case of the Spanish bank Popular. In France, its Spanish competitor Argentaria spoke French to its Spanish emigrant customers. Popular attacked this head-on, speaking Spanish to the emigrants in France and using the slogan 'Now you do not have to speak French to take care of your money'. More than just attacking a language problem, this addressed the historical rivalry between Spain and France. Touching this soft spot was highly successful.

And sometimes the weak spot is hidden in the competitor's operations and so must be dug out. Tylenol was counter-positioned to Aspirin, with the claim that it carried no risk of stomach bleeding. Lowenbrau's slogan against Beck's was: 'Now that you have tried the most popular German beer in the US, experience the most popular German beer in Germany'.

Finally, the competitor itself can occasionally provide the weak point. If you can turn the competitor's argument back on itself, take advantage of it. Faced with the Listerine slogan 'a mouthwash to kill all germs', the Scope brand attack was 'healthy breath without the taste and smell of a hospital'. A McDonald's ad that showed lettuce, tomato, onions, ketchup, and cheese floating down onto a bun prompted the Burger King attack 'where is the beef?'

The second issue when looking for the Achilles' heel is that not every weakness matters. And third, the weakness must be significant – the customer must care about it. Otherwise it will be irrelevant.

Take porcelain. It has an elegant image, associated with England, where the tradition of taking tea in elegant porcelain developed. Most US customers wrongly believed that Lenox Porcelain came from England. So Royal Doulton, a traditional English producer, advertised itself as 'Royal Doulton, the porcelain of Stoke-on-Trent from England', against Lenox, 'the porcelain from Pomona, New Jersey'.

Authentic vodka is associated with Russia. Stolichnaya was able to label Smirnoff, Samovar, and Wolfschmidt as phoney just by pointing out where they came from: Connecticut, Pennsylvania, and Indiana respectively.

Finally, we must make sure that when we attack our competitor, it cannot solve its weakness rapidly. Burger King's slogan 'Have it your way', which was an attack on McDonald's lack of flexibility, was not as successful as it could have been because McDonald's responded within a few months by offering burgers without onions, and/or cheese, and/or tomato, etc.

But Smirnoff cannot easily transfer its operations to Russia. So Stolichnaya's attack on inauthentic vodka is an effective one.

Figure 3.12 summarizes the five ways to find a weak point and the three major characteristics that this must have.

How to identify the weak spot	
I	Market research on clients
II	Social trends
III	Cultural issues
IV	Look at the competitor's operations
V	Turn the competitor's promotion on itself

Main charactersitics it must have	
I	Large
II	Highly relevant for clients
III	Not easy to solve

Figure 3.12 ◆ How to find the weak spot

Why do corporations tend to forget these important issues? They seem obvious. But egos frequently get in the way. And as Edgar Allan Poe said in *The Purloined Letter*, 'sometimes the obvious is the most difficult to see'.

And what is the obvious? That when making a frontal attack, we go against someone who is already there. The competitor may have been first in the segment, with all the prestige associated with being first to market. In any case the competitor will know the segment better than us. The size that counts is the size in the industry, not the total corporation size. The competitor will have market share advantages over us. So the burden of proof is on us – customers are likely to give the established competitor the benefit of doubt, rather than abandoning them for us.

The first three criteria can be summarized in one word when performing a frontal attack: focus. First concentrate on one market segment; then on only one competitor within it; then focus solely on one competitor weakness. This will make the frontal attack much more powerful (see Figure 3.13).

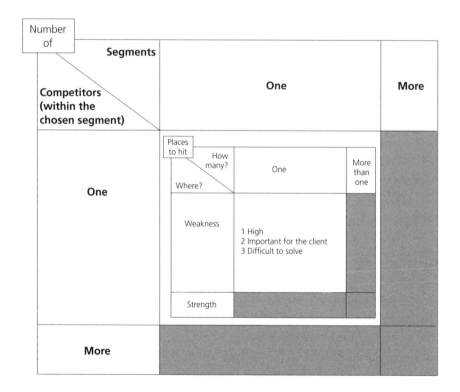

Figure 3.13 ◆ Finding the focus for a frontal attack

There are other rules that must be followed when performing a frontal attack. First we must have some kind of *competitive advantage*. (Obviously there is no point in attacking a competitor's weakness if we are still worse off.)

A competitive advantage can result from one of three sources. The first is that we may have *strengths that match success factors*. The first computers were invented by Univac in the fifties. IBM's mainframe hardware was pretty similar. But IBM's me-too product was able to dislodge Univac's market position because IBM offered much better software and service, in terms of installation, training, and maintenance.

Synergy can be a second source of competitive advantage. Gillette was able to attack Bic successfully in the disposable razors market because it benefited from the know-how, distribution channel, and image as a producer of other types of razors and related hygiene products.

Sometimes *size* helps. Napoleon used to say that God was on the side of the larger battalions. Size helped IBM against Apple in the PC segment. By emulating the distribution channels, the training program, and the promotions, IBM achieved 23 percent market share two years after entry.

The fifth and sixth rules are the importance of *surprise* (to prevent the competitor from being prepared) and the need to deploy resources *fast* (to give competitors no time to react). Fast resource deployment, on top of surprise, reinforce each other and take the competitor aback.

There is then a seventh criteria any frontal attack should follow. In war, an army soldier will fight with greater strength when trapped. So it is always better to leave the competitor *a way out*.

I once was at an industry conference where the CEO announced his plans to replace another competitor as the leader in a given market segment within five years. The competitor's CEO happened to be sitting next to me. Going pale and sitting stiffly in his seat, all he was able to mumble was, 'Over my dead body'. From that moment on, the fight between those two CEOs ceased to be about sales, market share, or profits. It became about saving face. One CEO could not back off, but the other could not afford to be defeated. Three years down the road, and millions down the drain, a vicious price war had left both corporations considerably worse off than they were at the beginning.

The lesson is, leave the competitor an escape route. Be sure it has other segments it can pull back to (so if you are fighting a specialist, prepare for a much harder struggle). And most especially leave their pride intact by not publicizing your attack.

Even when following the above seven rules, frontal attacks are sometimes unsuccessful and frequently costly. Therefore, the eighth rule is that you must be sure the attack is worth it in terms of *attractiveness*. Volume of sales, future growth rate, and eventual value (the profit margins) must outweight the cost of invested resources and the risk of being unsuccessful. For a summary of the eight rules see Figure 3.14

We can maximize our chances of success, and 'deserve success', in Churchill's words, but luck also plays a role – in business and war. As von Clausewitz once put it, 'war is the stage of uncertainty'.

We now move into the last two ways of attacking: undifferentiated circle and differentiated circle. They differ from all types of attack we have seen so far because they attack more than one segment.

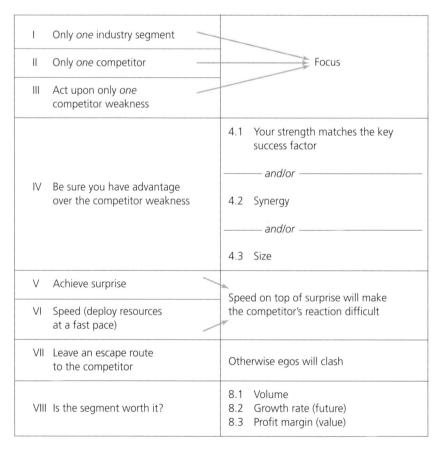

I	Only *one* industry segment	
II	Only *one* competitor	Focus
III	Act upon only *one* competitor weakness	
IV	Be sure you have advantage over the competitor weakness	4.1 Your strength matches the key success factor — *and/or* — 4.2 Synergy — *and/or* — 4.3 Size
V	Achieve surprise	Speed on top of surprise will make the competitor's reaction difficult
VI	Speed (deploy resources at a fast pace)	
VII	Leave an escape route to the competitor	Otherwise egos will clash
VIII	Is the segment worth it?	8.1 Volume 8.2 Growth rate (future) 8.3 Profit margin (value)

Figure 3.14 ◆ **Eight rules to follow in a frontal attack**

3.6 Undifferentiated circle

This attack's characteristics are threefold:

1 You enter a new industry and/or geographical area through more than one segment.

2 Those segments are similar to those that the leaders are in.

3 Among the different segments one tries to obtain synergy.

Figure 3.15 illustrates the concept of undifferentiated circles.

Examples of successful military circles are when the Carthaginian army surrounded the Romans at Cannae in 216 BC, the Zulus' buffalo horns tactic, and when the North Vietnamese surrounded the French army in Vietnam in 1954.

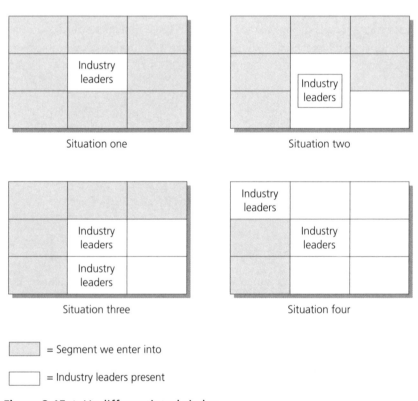

Figure 3.15 ◆ Undifferentiated circles

In business, Ivory is a good example. It produces both solid and liquid soaps. The solid soap is sold to several social class segments and to good quality health clubs, hotels, and restaurants. Its liquid version is standardized and focusses on average and above-average gyms, hotels, restaurants, coffee shops, and offices.

Ivory tries to serve all these several market segments with minimal differentiation. Both types of soap have the same content, and only the packaging is altered to suit different types of customer. The distribution channels and sales forces also change to suit different clients (see Figure 3.16).

Since the content of the soap is always the same, Ivory is able to benefit from large sale economies in manufacturing, and thus take advantage of synergies among the several segments it operates in.

That is the essence of an undifferentiated circle. One foot in one camp, another foot in a different one, but both close enough in order not to fall apart. This requires a high level of synergy among the segments. Synergy can be achieved by having fewer models than segments or as many models as segments, but the important fact is that the models are equal or at least similar to each other in terms of the characteristics that most influence scale economies. Synergy is at its highest (a) the more similar the models are among themselves, and (b) the lower the number of models, i.e.

Models How similar they are \ Number of	High	Low
High	Synergy increases →	(Maximum synergy)
Low	(Minimum synergy)	

So the components, new materials, and marketing are kept as constant as possible among all market segments. Differentiation comes from accessory characteristics – packaging, distribution, guarantee, level of service, and so on. Prudential, Sears, Texas Instruments, Lincoln Electric, Briggs & Stratton, and Wrangler are examples of undifferentiated circles. The lessons learned are always the same. Grab segments as much as you can, and differentiate models as little as possible. Be rigid in the essential product characteristics. Be flexible in the accessory ones.

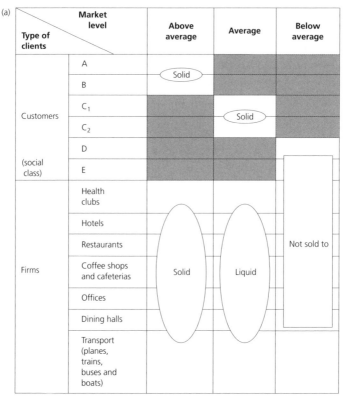

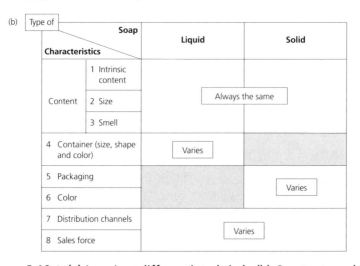

Figure 3.16 ◆ (a) Ivory's undifferentiated circle (b) Constants and variables in Ivory's strategy

This strategy is well illustrated by the old tale of the army cook who, when asked what there was for lunch, replied that, for the officers, there was Hungarian goulash (stewed pieces of meat with potatoes), for the sergeants' dining hall, veal cooked the gardener's way (again stewed pieces of meat with potatoes), and for the soldiers' mess, meat with potatoes. All served with different cutlery and crockery and in different dining halls.

The are two dangers associated with undifferentiated circles. First, there is the risk of over-extending our domain and thus becoming prey to specialists of the segments we operate in. This is what has been happening to Sears, increasingly confronted by so-called category killers (Toys R Us, Decathlon, Conforama, Staples, Worten, and so on).

Second, there is the danger of spreading our resources too thinly and making our presence in the various segments weak, even if our main competitors are not specialists.

In 1975 Coors Banquet was the market leader in beer share in 10 of the 11 US states it was sold in. Although distributed only in the west it had the fourth largest market share in the USA (after Budweiser, Schlitz, and Pebit).

Then Coors tried to surround its competitors by entering into new segments: light beer, dry beer, red beer, ice beer, non-alcoholic beer, extra-gold beer. Coors invented a series of new brands for this attack: Killian, Keystone, and Schulers.

What were the consequences of rolling out in so many directions? Today Coors is no longer the number one beer in any state. As it over-extended, it lost its leadership.

So undifferentiated circles must be implemented with great caution. There are seven rules to follow.

3.6.2 How to perform undifferentiated circles

The first rule is to ensure you have *synergy*. Resource sharing must occur among segments – for example in the sales force, transport, warehousing, the plant machinery, staff know-how, suppliers, quality control department, etc. It could be image – as Nestlé managed with its focus on food, both for adults (ice cream, chocolate) and babies (milk, food, and cereals).

Or it can be the distribution channels, which are common across skis, ski wear, tennis rackets, and casual sportive clothing for Head Ski Corporation.

It can be the plant workers' know-how, which is what led many Swiss watch makers to diversify into various sorts of precision instruments for the aviation industry.

In short, be it synergy in marketing (as in the case of Nestlé and Head Ski), or synergy in technical know-how (as with Swiss watch companies), the essential aspect is that, in order to obtain high synergy, a company must keep some kind of focus. Without focus, there is no high level synergy. And without synergy, diversification becomes risky.

Kodak, Compac, and Olivetti provide good examples of this. In the 1980s Kodak restructured five times, always in search of greater efficiencies. These never came, because Kodak had over-extended its product line into computers, batteries, household products, and even pharmaceuticals. Then a new CEO, George Fisher, decided to focus on image: 'imaging offers tremendous opportunities for long-term growth'. One of these growth areas was digital products. Kodak invested over $5 billion in research and development, of which the first major result was the photo CD.

Compac has never diversified into telecommunications, multimedia, or services, unlike Olivetti (the largest computer manufacturer after Siemens Nixdorf). The result? Not only does Compac consistently outperform Olivetti, but the latter has faced serious difficulties since 1990. Why? 'Olivetti used to do too many things', in the words of Corredo Passera, Olivetti's Managing Director.

So the first rule when surrounding a competitor is: *keep a focus*, so that there is relatedness among the several segments. The new segment will benefit in some way from the older one(s).

In order to obtain synergy it is useful to *minimize differentiation* in the technical core of the products, so that the technical know-how and product characteristics can be shared among the various segments. This is the second rule when performing an undifferentiated circle: keep the tangible aspects constant.

As we saw above, the differentiation comes from the intangibles – brand, design, distribution, service, etc.

The third rule concerns *brand name*. As long as segments are relatively similar, one name (encompassing both the corporation and the models) will do. As segments increase in numbers and/or differences, one name risks creating confusion in customers' minds. Then one should introduce one name for each model – in other words, develop a brand.

TAG Heuer uses the same name for several watch models because they are all basically similar.[12] Swatch kept the same name too, to begin with. But as it extended its line, it slowly introduced specific branding: the SKIN swatch; the Sea Dive line; the Sport line; and so on.

The fourth rule of undifferentiated circles is that one must be aware of the danger of *negative synergy* – the harmful impact of one segment into another. One source can be management interference, if knowledge and experience from one market is not directly applicable into another. Image can be another source of negative synergy. If you enter a high social class segment, the new product can be hurt by the image of the earlier, less luxurious one. Equally, if aiming for a lower social class, the new low-price version can damage the image of the more expensive product.

This is why Porsche discontinued its cheaper Volksporsche model. And when Rolex decided to market a relatively inexpensive watch, they called it Tudor, to disassociate it completely from the Rolex brand.

Image can even be a source of negative synergy when the models are not better or worse, but just different. Levi Strauss tried to transport Levi's name and image into the athletic apparel market, including ski wear and warm-up suits. Then into men's suits ('Levi's Action suits'), then into shoes, hats, and luggage. None of these extensions were successful.

Levi's learned its lesson – when it later extended to meet the trend for casual clothing in the workplace, it called its extension Dockers.

As a fifth rule, one must *avoid cannibalism* – our segments and models feeding on the sales of our other segments and models.

Model cannibalism is more likely if the company has fewer models in proportion to segments. Segment cannibalism is more likely when the segments are close. Häagen-Dazs' own retail shop sales suffered from huge supermarket sales – until the company came up with differentiated products specifically for the retail shops.[13]

So to avoid cannibalism, a company must manage both its segments and models by keeping price and product characteristics apart.

General Motors is a good example. Back in 1921, when Alfred Sloan took over the company, General Motors' pricing was chaotic, each product overlapping the other:

- ◆ Chevrolet: $795 to $2075
- ◆ Oakland: $1395 to $2065
- ◆ Oldsmobile: $1445 to $3300
- ◆ Scripps-Booth: $1545 to $2295
- ◆ Sheridan: $1685

◆ Buick: $1795 to $3295

◆ Cadillac: $3790 to $5690

With the slogan 'a car for every purse and purpose' Sloan selected the brands and the prices needed to dominate the automotive industry and avoid canni-balism. That involved distinguishing the price ranges, discarding a few brands (Scripps-Booth and Sheridan), and renaming Oakland as Pontiac:

◆ Chevrolet: $450 to $600

◆ Pontiac: $600 to $900

◆ Oldsmobile: $900 to $1200

◆ Buick: $1200 to $1700

◆ Cadillac: $1700 to $2500

Sloan got rid of price overlaps and no brand competed head-on against another. The internal expression at GM at the time was: 'Chevrolet is for the hoi polloi, Pontiac for the poor but proud, Oldsmobile for the comfortable but discreet, Buick for the striving, and Cadillac for the rich.'

By 1931, General Motors had captured 31 percent of the US market, over-taking Ford (with 28 percent) for the first time. For the next 50 years, GM's market share approached 50 percent.

When Sloan retired, however, his iron control disappeared. As a result, GM slowly went back to its old ways. More expensive Chevrolets and Ponti-acs were introduced, then Oldsmobile, Buick, and Cadillac came out in cheaper versions. Instead of maintaining their narrow focus, each General Motors division headed for the middle of the market where the sales volume was.

Today there are enormous price overlaps once more:

◆ Saturn: $9995 to $12,995

◆ Chevrolet: $8085 to $68,043

◆ Pontiac: $11,074 to $27,139

◆ Oldsmobile: $13,500 to $31,370

◆ Buick: $13,700 to $33,084

◆ Cadillac: $34,990 to $45,935

The most focussed divisions are Saturn (30 percent price range) and Cadillac (31 percent price range). These are also the two most successful divisions. The models that perform less well have larger price ranges, i.e. less focus. The highest priced Oldsmobile is 132 percent more expensive than the cheapest and for Buick the difference is 141 percent. Pontiac has a 145 percent difference and for Chevrolet it is an amazing 742 percent.

As George Santanyana wrote: 'Those who fail to remember the past are condemned to see it repeated'.

Circles mean line extensions. Any company performing them will pick fights with various competitors in several market segments. It will be much easier for us if those competitors are generally like us, i.e. not specialists.

Therefore the sixth rule is that when there is a choice, one should *opt for segments with a minimum of specialists*. Of course, that is not always possible, and the risk is that the specialists will outperform our (general) company, more than a general competitor would.

General Electric is a great name to sell all kinds of electric household products, and it is also a well-run company. Nevertheless, GE is not the market leader in several of its segments. In food processing, the leader is Cuisinart. In refrigerators, it is Frigidaire. Nor is GE the leader in washing machines (Maytag) or irons (Sunbeam). The only electric product where GE has consistently led is microwave ovens.

All these competitors are specialists, and this is why GE cannot break free of them. So follow the rule if you can – avoid markets full of specialists.

The seventh rule is to select the *most attractive segments*, in terms of value (unit margin), both now (current sales volume) and in the future (growth rate). Calvin Klein has achieved this in the perfume category, first with Obsession, then Escape, and, most recently, CK One. Black & Decker focussed itself on the DIY market, then introduced De Walt as a brand directed at the professional. Levi Strauss introduced Britannia as a discount line.

Finally, circles are easier to achieve if the segments you enter are *guerrillas or bypasses*, for the reasons explained above.

Figure 3.17 summarizes the eight rules that undifferentiated circles should follow. The first five of these rules can be summarized in one statement: make the total greater than the sum of the parts.

When enlarging product lines, companies will benefit if they are able to 'have a core of unity, be it either technology or market based', according to Peter Drucker. This reminds us that a chain is only as strong as its weakest link.

Strategy is *sacrifice* – this is indicated by the last three rules (avoid specialists, avoid unattractive segments, and avoid head-on battles). Without sacrifice, strategy does not exist. The most important strategic word is *no* – sacrifice means giving up something in order be successful elsewhere.

I	Search for synergy	
II	Differentiate intangibles (image, service) and keep tangibles (product/technological core) constant	
III	Manage the brand names according to the number and relatedness of the segments	Total greater than the sum of parts
IV	Be aware of the risk of negative synergy	
V	Avoid cannibalism through proper management of price ranges and product characteristics	The strength of a chain is the strength of its weakest link
VI	Opt for segments with few specialists	
VII	Select the most attractive segments	
VIII	Select segments which are guerrillas or bypasses, not flankings	

Figure 3.17 ◆ **Rules for implementing undifferentiated circles**

3.7 The differentiated circle

This is the most difficult attack, since one enters into a new industry and/or geographical area with the following characteristics:

◆ You enter more than one segment.

◆ A distinctive model is offered for each segment.

◆ No attempt is made to obtain synergy among the models and segments.

The models in the various segments are on their own: they do not share scale costs, experience, know-how, or image. Because of this, market power is also limited. Our company behaves less as a unique whole and more as several smaller parts.

Boeing is a good example of this type of strategy. It offers the 737 model for short-range travel, the 727 for medium range, the 720 for continental travel, the 707 for intercontinental journeys, the 747 for largest capacity, and so on. Coca-Cola is another example – Classic Coke, caffeine free, Diet Coke, Cherry Coke, etc.

Vlasic Foods owns regional pickles brands with distinctive characteristics, American Express is a highly differentiated bank, and Honda uses the differentiated circle with its brands: Civic, Prelude, Accord, Stream, Accura, NSX, etc. IBM employs it with its motto: 'Our strength is the fact that we make everything; whatever you need, we've got it: PCs, micros, minis, super-minis, mainframes, mini super computers, work stations, software layers, and all other types of software.'

So the philosophy of companies performing differentiated circles is that there is a firm for all, but not equal to all.

To visualize the differentiated circle in military terms, consider the two round barricades that Julius Caesar erected during the Gallic Wars: one internal barricade to keep Vercingetorix and the Gauls confined to the town of Aletia, and an external wall to keep the Gallic relieving forces out.

There are basically three *sources of failure* in differentiated circles: the number of segments one is in; the fact that one aims at having as many models as segments; and the need for a good match between segments and models. Differentiated circles stand better chances of success if five principles are followed.

3.7.1 Five principles for differentiated circles

First there must be a *good overlap* between each model and its segment. This begins with the brand name, which should indicate what the model stands for. Realemon is a natural drink with lemon extract. General Electric, Miller Lite, Vision Center, and Superglue are all brands that state clearly what the product does. As do the magazines *Fortune, Business Week, People, Sail,* and *Yachting.*

As well as the name, all other model characteristics must fit well with the segment requirements. Sara Lee's pantyhose L'Eggs comes in different colors, is packaged in an attractive white plastic egg, is reasonably priced, and is distributed through supermarkets. Appealing to the practical, low-priced market, Sara Lee does not target department stores but supermarkets – where women who want to buy everyday hosiery shop regularly.

So that there is a good fit between a given segment and its model, it is also important that all model characteristics reinforce each other. Dove is a soap that focusses on the women's beauty segment – the price, size, and cleaning attributes are not emphasized. The box is similar to cosmetics boxes, not simply paper wrapping. The soap itself is oval and creamy, emphasizing that it creates lots of foam. And the 'Dove love' message is created by the advertising slogan: 'Dove creams your skin while you wash'. The model characteristics reinforce each other – union makes strength.

Third, in order to reinforce each model's focus on a specific segment, one must clearly *differentiate* between the various models.[14]

Again, differentiation begins with the name, which allows for distinctive advertising, and ends with all the model's other characteristics: type of product, price, and need.

Name differentiation is illustrated by *Time*. When the magazine launched a business magazine, it did not call it *Time Business*, but *Fortune*. Similarly the pictures magazine was called *Life*, not *Time Pictures*, and the money magazine was called *Money*, not *Time Finance*. *Entertainment Weekly* and *People* came next, rather than *Time Entertainment* or *Time Celebrities*, and so on.

Vendôme is a good example of differentiation based on product types. It develops and acquires brands that meet its definition of luxury. The company brands include Alfred Dunhill men's products, Mont Blanc pens, Sulka ties, Karl Lagerfeld designs, Cartier jewellery, Baume & Mercier and Piaget watches, and others.

Price differentiation is used by Gillette, which dominates the wet shaving industry, and by Anheuser-Busch, which created a beer ladder with Busch, Budweiser, and Michelob.

An example of need differentiation is Darden restaurants with their two chains: Red Lobster and Olive Green. Between the two, Darden covers seafood and Italian cuisine, two of the most popular types of food in the USA.

Fourth, the model chosen to enter into a segment must have strengths equal to the segment's success factors, otherwise it will face a competitive disadvantage.

Texas Instruments invented the integrated circuit in 1958 and benefits from hundreds of millions of dollars a year in royalties generated by its semiconductor patents. Rather than focussing on where it had competitive advantage, TI entered into consumer electronics, then personal computers, laptop computers, minicomputers and software, digital watches, and so on. Most of these ventures were unsuccessful. The minicomputer and digital watch divisions were closed down. The doomed home computer segment cost Texas Instruments $600 million in losses.

The fifth rule is to *enter in strength*, to offset two disadvantages our company possesses. First, the segment we enter into is new. Second, there is no synergistic resource sharing between it and others: our strategy is based on model differentiation. Thus, size of entry will provide our company with some potential leverage: scale economies, experience effects, and market share power. However, since the benefits of scale, experience, and share are frequently segment-specific, the size that matters most is the size within each segment, not the total company size.

Exxon is by any measure (sales, total assets, or market capitalization) larger than IBM or Xerox. But for a decade Exxon tried without success to surround IBM and Xerox in the office automation market. It relentlessly brought out digital systems, computer screens, telephone-answering systems, advanced work stations, disk systems with optic memory, semi-conductor lasers, and so on. Exxon spread its resources so thinly in the various segments of office automation that it was never able to create a sufficiently robust bridge to enter, let alone dominate, any of them.

If it is vital for large companies within a single industry to enter in strength, it is especially important when the total size of the firm is smaller than other industry competitors (and most specially when line extension means diversification into other industries not in the same industry). American Motors is a good example of the first scenario, and Hallmark of the second.

After its formation in 1954 and until its sale to Chrysler Corporation in 1987, American Motors was always much smaller than the big three – GM, Ford and Chrysler. So it would have made sense to focus on a small part of the industry where the big three were weaker: subcompacts and compacts. Alternatively, American Motors could have exploited the opportunites provided by the Jeep. In the 1970s, the Jeep accounted for more sales than any other type of American Motors car and was profitable, whereas all of AM's other cars lost money.

However, American Motors opted to do the opposite: it pursued product extension to become a full-line car manufacturer. Instead of doing fewer things better, AM added to its problems: it brought out the luxury Ambassador, several convertibles, mini-vans, the Alliance, the Encore, and the Fuego. By 1986 the only asset left at American Motors was the accumulated losses providing a $500 million tax shelter. The next year (1987) Chrysler bought American Motors and stopped producing everything except the Jeep. Within a few years Jeep sales had more than doubled.

The lesson? Fewer models (and segments) does not necessarily mean lower sales – on the contrary, since fewer means stronger, fewer also means more.

If that is true when extending the line within an industry, it is especially true when diversifying among industries. Take Hallmark. It successfully extended its line within the boundaries of the greetings card industry. There was a classic Hallmark line, the Ambassador line for discounters, the Shoebox line of humorous cards, and the Pet Love line for pet owners. All these line extensions did well financially. But then it moved into jewellery (Trifari), printing (Litho-Krume), picture frames (Burnes of Boston), Spanish-language TV (Univision), and so on – including bizarre trips into the world of cable TV productions and real estate. The result? A financial fiasco. 'Can Hallmark get well soon?' asked the headline of an article in *Business Week*, 19 June 1995.

The sixth rule with differentiated circles is *follow the money*. As the riskiest of all strategies, the segments one enters into must be attractive (in terms of sales, margin, and growth). Remember: the essence of strategy is sacrifice.[15] And the most important word in strategy is no – defining where I am *not* going to be.

3.7.2 Synthesis

The increasing purchasing power and sophistication of customers leads to market fragmentation. Industries divide themselves more and more. Computers originally meant one segment – mainframes – but now there are laptops, micro-computers, minicomputers, super computers used by NASA, etc.

In the first years of American television, ABC, CBS, and NBC had 90 per cent market share. But today there is Network TV, Independent TV, Cable, Pay, Public Service, Interactive, and so on.

The phenomenon of market fragmentation helps firms develop differentiated circles. That's the positive side of this strategy. But there is also a negative side. First, management becomes more difficult as the number of segments increases. Second, companies following this strategy abdicate from synergy to maximize differentiation. This creates another type of difficulty, called *model management*:

- Ensuring that segments and models overlap.
- Making sure that each model's characteristics reinforce each other.
- Driving incremental model differentiation.

The difficulty of model management plus the risk of line over-extension makes differentiated circles the most difficult of all types of attack. The objective is to reach a large number of new customers, but there is the risk of ending up with lots of people who do not buy.

Figure 3.18 emphasizes the rules to follow.

I	Model and segment must overlap
II	All models' characteristics must reinforce each other
III	Force differentiation among models
IV	Ensure that your model has strengths that match the segment's success factors
V	Entry into each segment must be in strength
VI	Segment must be worthwhile in terms of: • unit margin • sales volume • growth rate

Figure 3.18 ◆ Achieving a differentiated circle

3.8 Summary

In this chapter, six types of attack strategy were analyzed:

1 Guerilla.

2 Bypass.

3 Flanking attack.

4 Frontal attack.

5 Undifferentiated circle.

6 Differentiated circle.

There are essentially three distinct characteristics to remember (see Figure 3.19). First, strategies 1–4 concern entry in one segment only. Strategies 5 and 6 concern entry into two or more segments. Second, strategies 1–2

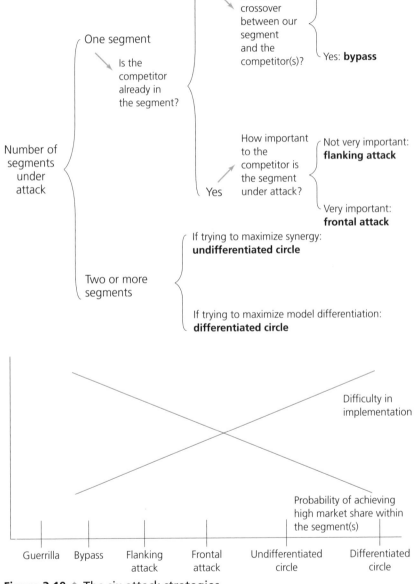

Figure 3.19 ◆ The six attack strategies

concern entry into a segment where there is no competition present. Strategies 3–4 enter segments where there is competition. Third, probability of success declines with each strategy. Guerrilla attacks stand the highest chance of success; the differentiated circle strategy is the hardest to achieve high market share in. (This does not mean that the differentiated circle is not worth considering – when the criteria of Figure 3.18 are met, it can be the right thing to do.)

In general, all of the attack strategies are harder to do well than the defense strategies. Here, the disadvantages of the attacker (lack of segment experience, lower market share, etc.) are the advantages of the defender.

4

Defense: the eight strategic movements

"This animal is very wicked: when it is attacked it defends
itself."

Théodore P. K., La Ménagerie

"Those who defend everything, defend nothing."
Ferdinand Foch, Marshal of France, Principles of War

4.1 Introduction

THERE ARE ESSENTIALLY eight defense strategies:

1 Signaling.

2 Creating entry barriers (fixed and mobile).

3 Global service.

4 Pre-emptive strike.

5 Blocking.

6 Counter-attack.

7 Holding the ground.

8 Withdrawal.

If attack = entry + unprovoked, defense is a strategy where one of these two elements is absent. In three strategies (1, 2 and 7) the company does not enter a new market, but 'stands still' – signaling, creating entry barriers (fixed or mobile), or simply holding the ground.

Alternatively, the company does enter a new market (industry, geographical area, or segment), but does so as a reaction to a competitor. Strategies 3, 4, 5, 6 and 8 are this type of defense.

Signaling and creating entry barriers are the earliest possible strategies to follow. Global service broadens the offering to prevent customers going elsewhere. This is similar to strategies 1 and 2, the only difference being that it involves entry into new segments.

If these three strategies cannot be implemented or they fail, the earliest possible strategy is the pre-emptive strike – move before the competitor does. Blocking can be implemented as the competitor attacks or shortly afterwards; the counter-attack comes after the competitor has moved; and holding the ground is the equivalent of standing still. Withdrawal should only be considered if all else fails.

Defense strategies are more likely to succeed than attacks, since the attacker's disadvantages are the defender's advantages.

The defender may have been first to market and so its brand is associated with the product in the customer's mind – Aspirin, Coca-Cola, Xerox, Black & Decker, Band-aid, Gillette, Jeep, Kodak, Kleenex, and so on.

Even if that is not the case, the defender has other advantages over the attacker: greater market know-how (of suppliers, distribution channels, technology, and clients' psychology), market share (and thus visibility and image), experience benefits (learning curve), and possibly larger scale and synergy.[1]

Finally, most people are risk averse and so will stick to the established product when in doubt. The newcomer must provide arguments strong enough to persuade the customer to change – lower price, greater quality, faster delivery. (Some customers – early adopters – try new things because they are new. But they are the exception, not the rule.)

However, as we saw in Chapter 3, although the odds are in favor of the defender, if the attacker follows certain rules it may well succeed. Therefore, rather than merely being passive, the defender must attempt to minimize the attacker's chances of success. Figure 4.1 illustrates the eight defense strategies a defender can use.

(a)

Types of strategy	No movement	Movement occurs (entry or exit of a segment)	
		Entry	Exit
1 Signaling	✓		
2 Creating entry barriers	✓		
3 Offer global service		✓	
4 Pre-emptive strike		✓	
5 Blockage		✓	
6 Counter-attack		✓	
7 Holding the ground	✓		
8 Withdrawal			✓

(b)

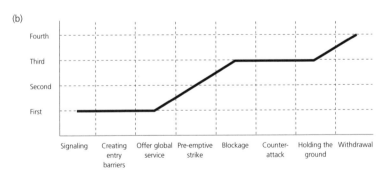

Figure 4.1 ◆ (a) The eight defense strategies (b) Sequence in which the eight types of defense should be considered

4.2 Signaling

The main objective of signaling is to warn the enemy not to enter our market and thus to obtain the best of all victories: one without a fight. We can save money, time, and other resources if a warning is enough to deter a competitor from entering our market. Sun Tzu put expressed it this way: 'the supreme act of war is to subdue the enemy without fighting'.[2]

Intimidation was frequently used by Napoleon. He made a point of showing himself in front of his troops before battles, so that the enemy could see him. Wellington acknowledged after defeating Napoleon at Waterloo, 'His presence in a battle was worth forty thousand soldiers'.

Mao Tse-tung cultivated an enigmatic personality, making a point of being perceived incoherent and contradictory, demonstrating the power of intimidation in politics.

In business, there are various ways to signal a competitor that we will, if necessary, defend our market forcefully. We can increase factory capacity, creating the prospect in the competitor's mind of flooding the market with cheaper products if the competitor decides to enter it. This is a costly signaling strategy, but there are cheaper ones too. We could swap board members with a financial institution, and convey a message of having financial backing for whatever war lies ahead.

Messages can be verbalized or not, and can be directed at customers or competitors, within our segment or outside it.

An example of a message targeting customers is IBM's practice of announcing new computer series two or three years before launch. This tactic is designed to prevent customers buying competitors' models in the meantime.

Texas Instruments provides an example of signaling to competitors by deeds not words. In the 1980s TI announced a price for random access memory (RAM) chips to be marketed in 1983. A week later, Bowmar counter-offered a lower price for RAM chips with the same characteristics. Motorola followed that with an even lower price three weeks later.

What did TI do? Two weeks after Motorola's offer, TI called a press conference and announced a new price half that offered by Motorola. Both Motorola and Bowmar got the message – TI would undercut any price. To prove it, TI priced its chips at half the price of the cheapest competitor, and used the media to cement the commitment in its competitors' minds. This tactic was double-edged – any retreat would mean total loss of face. Like Cortez when he arrived in Mexico, TI burned its ships, leaving no escape. The struggle would be to the death.

When signaling to firms *outside* our segment, the objective is to deter entry. IMS has been able to deter competitors from entering the pharmacy and hospital information market for drug products on virtually a worldwide basis (the exception is AZYX, which only operates in a few countries). But sometimes the strategy does not work. AC Nielsen, with the largest share in US grocery sales and television audience measurement, has been unable to deter competition. AGB, Times Sales Area Marketing, McGraw-Hill's Data Resources, and Control Data's Arbitron subsidiaries were not deterred by Nielsen and all successfully penetrated its US markets.

Therefore, whichever type of deterrent is used, there are some rules that will maximize the chances of success.

4.2.1 How to signal

First, make sure that your commitment is known. Texas Instruments used a press conference; an interview in the press or on primetime television would also work. Or you can make a statement in the annual report, a speech at an industry conference, and so on. Basically, the idea is to *publicize* one's determination.

Second, publicity must be directed towards those companies that *matter most*. They are not the direct competitors already within our segment. They are the indirect competitors – those in industry segments other than ours. Messages should also be directed at firms outside our industry that have the resources to succeed in it. Finally, signaling should also be directed at anyone we suspect to be considering entry – assuming they are companies that have what it takes to be a serious competitor. Figure 4.2 illustrates this.

In order to identify indirect competitors, one must focus on the need served, not the product manufactured. If we manufacture glass bottles, then producers of plastic bottles, cans, and cardboard are all indirect competitors. To identify potential entrants from outside our industry we need to know what resources are essential for success in our segment, which companies outside our segment and industry have the right type and sufficient quantity of those resources, and what the competitors' objectives and mission are.

For example, steel production yields sulphuric acid as a by-product, which makes steel companies potential candidates to enter the chemical industry too. The R&D of pharmaceutical companies is useful for developing cosmetics, creating a temptation for pharmaceutical companies to enter cosmetics. Manufacturing facilities for breakfast cereals can be used also to produce pet foods.

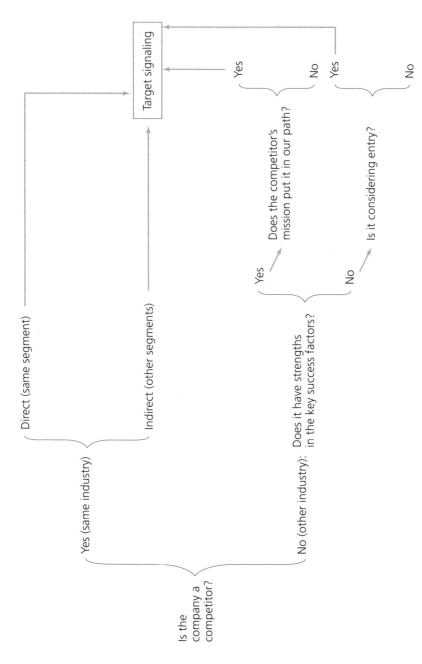

Figure 4.2 ◆ Identifying the companies to signal to

Since 'banking is where the customer is', according to the former CEO of Union des Banques Suisses, several retailers have branched into financial services (Sears, Pingo Doce). And so on.

It is also important to look at each competitor's mission. Depending upon how this is defined, the company will act differently under the same set of circumstances. We must detect what is at the root of a competitor's strategy in order to anticipate its various behaviors. For example, Toyota wants to become 'the world's largest car company', whereas Honda's mission is to develop superior engine technology; Honda's founder wanted to produce 'engines for the world'.

Kimberly-Clark and Procter & Gamble provide another example. Both companies are in the diapers (nappies) business with their Huggies and Pampers brands. But each is there for a different reason. Kimberly-Clark wants to optimize the capacity of its paper mills, and diapers is one market where it can do this. P&G, however, wants to 'meet the household needs of housewives', which is why it has broadened from groceries into the diapers market.

Third, our message must be *credible*. Credibility requires us to possess three qualities. We must have a reputation of fulfilling our promises. We must be seen as having the strength to retaliate, and our message must be coherent.

Competitors will easily see through your plans if you are not credible. VFW-Fokker, signaled to British Aerospace (BAe) that it would not tolerate BAe's plans to develop the HS-146 aircraft, because it would be in direct competition with Fokker's F-28 short-haul jet airliner. Fokker said publicly that over 40 percent of the total cost of both their F-27 and F-28 aircraft was supplied by British companies and that this injection into British industry was at risk if the HS-146 project went ahead. However, BAe correctly reasoned that the threat was not credible, since re-design, re-tooling, and re-certification costs for both aircraft using non-British equipment would be prohibitive to Fokker. So BAe went ahead with its HS-146 project.

The fourth rule is never to *humiliate* an individual who works for a competitor. Business must be rational and humiliation brings emotion into the arena. Whatever our threats, they should always be general and never directed against anyone specifically.

Fifth, signaling should be made before the potential entrant has made a full commitment to attack our market segment. After that, it is better to pretend not to know about it, and concentrate instead on preparing a surprise.

Finally, we will be more successful if signaling is accompanied by creating barriers to entry and implementing global service – our next two defense strategies.

4.3 Barriers to entry

This is the second means of defense, and involves creating obstacles that are difficult to overcome and thus discourage the competitor's entry into our market segment. There are five main points to note about barriers to entry.

First, like signaling, barriers to entry are a means of dissuasion. The message is the same: 'there is no point in joining our market, because you will have difficulty in succeeding in it.'

The principal difference is that signaling is usually verbalized. Entry barriers are created by action – creating an obstacle that needs to be overcome.

Second, we can attach a motto to barriers to entry: 'They shall not pass'. This was Marshal Pétain's statement to his French troops at Verdun in 1916 when the German army threatened to enter Paris.[3]

Third, as with any other strategy, barriers to entry can succeed and fail. Pétain succeeded at Verdun. But the Maginot Line in World War II failed. The German army bypassed it.

There are two types of entry barrier: *fixed* and *mobile*.

4.3.1 Fixed barriers to entry

Fixed barriers are stable obstacles – fortifications that the defender builds that the aggressive entrant has to overcome if it is to join the market. These barriers can be built in any business administration area: marketing, finance, accounting, manufacturing, etc. (see Figure 4.3).

Fixed barriers can be summarized as two major types: *tangible* and *intangible*.

Dow Chemical's heavy investment in raw materials to ensure it has a large supply of petrochemicals at the most advantageous prices is an example of a tangible fixed barrier. Another example is Coca-Cola, which started using fructose corn sweetener as a replacement for sugar in the 1980s, in order to gain a 20 percent cost saving. To stop its competitors following suit, Coke signed long-term purchase contracts with fructose suppliers, to tie up most of the supply.

Customer loyalty is an example of an intangible entry barrier. Customer loyalty has secured Cray's exclusive hold on the supercomputer segment of the computer industry. Cray generates this loyalty by building supercomputers to a very personalized specification. And Rolex has an intangible entry barrier – image. By indicating how time-consuming and expensive the products are to

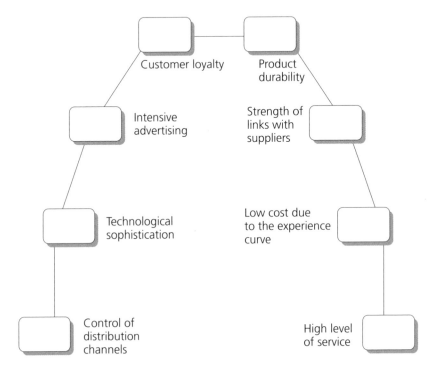

Figure 4.3 ◆ Fixed barriers to entry

make, Rolex creates a barrier to competitors wanting to enter its premium field.

Figure 4.4 shows the sequence of steps to follow when trying to create entry barriers.

The first step is to try to create *legal or technical difficulties* to entrants. These can be patents (pharmaceutical industry), or legal intervention by the government (for example to safeguard quality standards in food). The minimum reward you are aiming for is to postpone the newcomer's entry. A better result is to soften the competitor's effects (by forcing it to raise prices for instance) and the best result would be to forbid its market entry by legal means.

The second step is to increase your *market share* as quickly as possible. This can bring one or more of the following gains: lower cost due to larger size; lower cost due to experience (the learning curve);[4] better image (usually associated with larger sales) and strengthened relations with suppliers and/or retailers. P&G tried to use Tide to enter south European markets dominated

1	**Lobby** for legal and technical barriers
2	Build **market share** at the fastest possible pace
3	Concentrate the budget, top management, and best people on the variables that are **success factors**
4	Move down the **experience curve**
5	Maximize sharing among segments in order to optimize **synergy**

Figure 4.4 ◆ A step-by-step approach to building fixed barriers

by Unilever's Omo in the early 2000s. But Unilever used its influence in the distribution channels to make P&G's entrance as difficult as possible.

Nestlé stocks products at very low promotional prices in retail outlets as soon as it knows that a new competitor is about to enter into the market (in geographic or in product terms). This decreases retailer's space for the new product and thus minimizes its chances of being accepted by them.

The pace at which market share is built depends on the concentration of resources (to advertise and promote heavily, to invest in product development, to keep prices low). This, in turn, depends on each firm's specialization level. For example, Zippo, the original wind-proof lighter, was invented by George Blaisdell in 1932. Three hundred million lighters later, Zippos still have the same basic characteristics – there are no plastic Zippos or designer Zippos. In a world of change, Zippo stuck to its traditional segment. It invested heavily in promoting the guarantee ('if any Zippo lighter fails to work, we will fix it free') and in developing the quality, durability, and resistance of its product. The results? In the 1990s, the average annual sales growth rate exceeded 20 percent.

However, instead of perfecting their business and milking their cash cows, some companies invest their scarce resources in change for change's sake. When they do this, the pace of market share growth usually fails to be what it could.

Another type of barrier entry is to *concentrate on your key success factors*.

Key success factors are those tasks that are especially important for competitive success. The success factors for large custom-built air or gas compressors, for instance, would be as follows:

◆ Product development (satisfying customer specifications demonstrates that each compressor is unique).

◆ Image.

◆ The sales force's technical knowledge, enabling the company to sell highly complex and thus potentially dangerous products.

◆ Level of service (to minimize non-operational time).

◆ The technical knowledge of the factory work force.

These represent the variables where excellence is required, and which change from market segment to market segment. Therefore, erect entry barriers, and concentrate on your key success factors rather than building quality in 30 or 40 less important variables. Most of your *budget*, the best of your *people*, and the largest share of top management's *time* should be concentrated on those variables (see Figure 4.5(a)). In addition, the departments that handle these success factors should report directly to top management (see Figure 4.5(b)).

The fourth type of entry barrier is the *experience curve*. In some industries, unit costs decrease sharply as the cumulative volume of production increases, regardless of the firm's size: there is a learning curve for the work force and also for its supervisors. Firms learn which parts of the product give less value to the customer, and thus can make savings in these areas. Lower costs mean lower prices, which increases demand, decreases cost, and enables further reductions in price at no loss of profit.

Texas Instruments' success with the experience curve strategy in achieving the lowest delivered cost position was such that by 1977 it had gained market leadership in the personal calculator market – a position it held until the 1980s by maintaining its cost leadership strategy. Similar results were achieved by Bausch & Lomb in soft lenses, Briggs and Stratton in fractional horsepower motors, and Swedish Match in disposable cigarette lighters. Cost leadership can provide position defense in other businesses, such as electronic consumer goods retailers: 47th Street Photo in New York, Comet in the UK, and Eschen-Moser in Switzerland.

A firm should take four actions in order to move rapidly along its experience curve. First, create an *incentive system* to reward workers and supervisors. Second, as a separate programme and with distinct rewards, establish the *process analysis* by which the elements that provide less customer value are identified and their costs minimized. Third, develop a sophisticated *R&D department* and dedicate a considerable part of the budget to process. Finally, divide the R&D process into *applied* and *basic*. Applied R&D enables a firm to move rapidly along its learning curve. Basic R&D allows the creation of new learning curves below the previous ones.

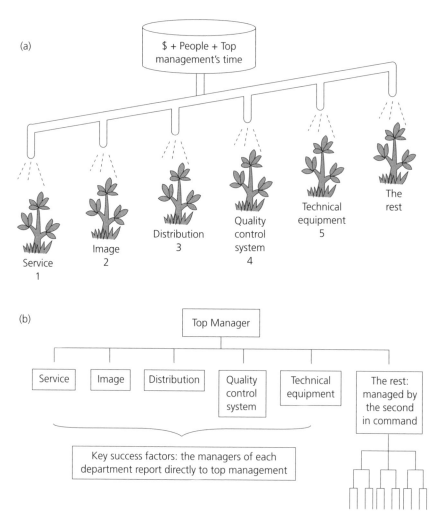

Figure 4.5 ◆ How to create excellence in the key success factors

Having high levels of *synergy* is a sixth type of entry barrier. Synergy occurs when the firm can share some resources because of similarities in the segments, e.g. factory, warehouse and transportation logistics, suppliers, or distribution channels.

For example, General Electric uses the same sales force to sell various types of electronic products: transformers, cables, switches, etc. Matsushita Electric shares its distribution channels among several types of electronic appliances: TVs, stereos, radios, and so on.

4.3.2 Mobile barriers

Mobile barriers are a new generation of products launched periodically, in the hope that their innovative qualities will discourage potential entrants who are not sure to be able to keep up the pace. They offer the defender a flexible response to attack and hence a way of taking the initiative. Mobile defense is sometimes known as active defense, as opposed to passive defense (fixed barriers).

McDonald's frequently introduces new products to spice up its business. These range from sandwiches to desserts, drinks, and sauces. Casio emphasizes product replacement, which is designed to shorten and accelerate product life cycles, in order to protect its position as a leading manufacturer of pocket calculators. And Abbot Laboratories has successfully defended its share for the generic erythromycin antibiotic by introducing a series of substitute products, such as erythromycin stearate, ethinyl succinate, and a series of dosage formulae, to target a variety of needs from the paediatric market for full dose applications. Abbott's mobile defense supported its high-priced products and defeated attacks by cheaper substitutes.

There are three questions that we should ask regarding mobile defenses. The first is, 'Are we not cannibalizing our own sales by launching a new generation of product before the previous one is obsolete?' The answer is yes – but it is preferable to displace your own sales, especially if you can upgrade margins as well as the product, than have a competitor do it.

Most firms learn this the hard way. Growth of Izod's Alligator brand was phenomenal in the USA for a few years. It became a hot fashion item and Izod could not produce enough shirts to meet demand. But then its sales started to decline. A number of clones appeared to fill market demand – competitors brought out fox, tiger, and horse brands. Izod also failed to capitalize on Alligator's popularity by updating the brightly colored sportswear that was the core of the brand's appeal. When pastel colors and stripes became the fashion, Izod stuck to its old line. Meanwhile the clones moved quickly to meet the changing fashion, marketing a complete line of shirts, sweaters, trousers, and accessories in the newly favored style. This depressed Izod's sales.

Gillette also learned the hard way. It dominated the shaving tools market with its Blue and Superblue brands. But then it allowed Wilkinson Sword to innovate steel blades. Gillette's market share decreased dramatically, only recovering when Gillette launched its own stainless steel model and moved fast to offer improved versions of its models, one after the other: Trac II, Atra Pivot, Sensor, Excel, Mach 3.

The second question to ask is, 'Is this type of defense not more appropriate in young industries?' Yes. Industries in the early stages of the life cycle are more easily defended by this strategy But this does not mean that it will not work for mature industries.

To do this, you must enlarge the notion of 'product' to encompass a larger concept: the offering (see Chapter 3, Section 3.5, undifferentiated circles). This encompasses service, delivery and all other elements of the value chain.

Improving *service* enabled GE's turbine division to increase its revenues from $2.2 billion in 1994 to $3 billion in 1996, a 36 percent increase in only two years. GE's turbine division shifted focus from selling to servicing – previously it sold 50 or so new gas turbines, but now it concentrated on servicing 10,000 existing turbines and 9000 jet engines. Much the same happened in GE's nuclear power division.

Innovation can also occur in *delivery*, as when Wal-Mart agreed to link its cash register data with GE's lighting division. This allowed for fast replacement of light bulbs on Wal-Mart shelves with minimal paperwork.

Japanese companies utilized the fact that mobile defense is free of boundaries to create a dominant position in a wide spectrum of industries: copying machines; semi-conductors; air-conditioning; electronics; robotics; photography; machine tools; and even steel textiles and ship building.

The third question to ask is, 'How do we create mobile barriers?'

There are four key ways. First, value analysis is vital – the whole value chain should be analyzed, not just the product core, to discover ways of innovating to create greater customer value.

Second, rules should be set for the rhythm at which product innovation will be launched. Three types of rule are usually followed, ranging from less severe to more demanding. The less severe rule requires new models to be launched when sales growth approaches zero, meaning that the market enters its mature phase of its life cycle. More demanding is the rule that requires an innovative model to be offered when the market's annual sales growth rate starts decelerating; increase is still positive, but the rate is slower.

The most demanding rule of all states that new models should be offered every two or three years.

Which rule is followed depends on how attractive our segment is and the strength of the potential competitor. The larger they both are, the more we should look at the more demanding rules.

The third key issue is that innovations must be *difficult to imitate*. Otherwise, they will not discourage entry and so not be a very effective barrier.

Fourth, it sometimes pays to announce the arrival of the new model in advance – as we saw earlier, this is a tactic IBM uses to discourage customers from switching to competitors. Such an announcement should only be made if a competitor is about to enter, or has already introduced a rival product.

4.3.3 Barriers: conclusion

Together with signaling, fixed or mobile barriers are useful defense tactics. But they do not always succeed. Sometimes it is too late for competitors to reverse their decision. At other times the segment is attractive enough for competitors to put aside their doubts and enter, even though we have defended our territory.

In such cases, there is the need for another type of defense strategy that can deter competitors from entering our segment: global service.

4.4 Global service

Global service is not the same as globalization – serving a worldwide market with a single model, creating efficiencies such as providing a worldwide product with a single marketing campaign. Global service is a separate, distinct concept. It refers to a company enlarging its product portfolio because the client prefers to buy from a single global supplier. To begin with, the customer defines the product more broadly than the supplier. Later, the supplier enlarges the offering to fit the customer's definition of the product.

For example, a company might prefer to buy all of its packaging from a single supplier: glass, plastic, metal, paper; large and small. In such a case, the supplier can either enlarge its portfolio of packaging, or risk losing the customer to a competitor who is prepared to enlarge its portfolio.

Banking and sanitation are two industries where global service is paramount. In banking, there used to be a clear difference between commercial banks, investment banks, and insurance companies. Those involved in one segment stayed clear of the others, sometimes for legal reasons. Nowadays the situation is entirely the reverse. A single financial institution will provide traditional commercial banking offerings (loans and account services), as well as brokerage services, asset management, insurance, and pensions. The result is one-stop banking, i.e. global service.

In basic sanitation, it is increasingly common to see the same supplier responsible for design, civil construction, equipment supply, and plant management – the design, construction, and operation are all controlled by the same turn-key contract.

We see the same situation in electronic consumer goods,[5] computers, etc. And some large auditing firms have enlarged their offering to include accounting, taxation, personnel selection, information technology, and so on.

4.4.1 A few points to note about global service

First, although we enter new segments, global service is a defense strategy, not an attack. This is because we enter new segments in order to protect our position in the old ones.

Second, global service is not the same as creating barriers to entry – barriers to entry do not involve entering new segments. Racal Electronics bought Decca because it possessed electronic warfare systems and microwave-frequency radios, product lines that Racal needed to fill holes in its coverage of the military communications market. Most of Racal's clients were governments who wanted one supplier to provide all their military electronics needs. Becoming a global service provider with the acquisition of Decca enabled Racal to broaden its portfolio, increase its total share of individual contracts, and reduce the inefficient method of building consortiums of companies with complementary products.

Third, we should attempt global service only if the customer cares significantly about it. If not, consider alternative defenses.

4.4.2 Rules for successful global service

There are two rules for successful global service. First, the customer should decide what the company includes in its enlarged portfolio. The customer defines what it lacks and where it prefers simplicity (of negotiating with a single supplier) over expertise (provided by specialists). Criteria the customer specifies when asking for bids and questions asked at the negotiating table are indicators of the customer's desires. Follow these wishes.

Second, the limits of product portfolio enlargement are set by one of two things. Credibility may decline when the company over-stretches – such as when banks tried to sell car-rental services inside the branches. The second limitation is when it becomes too difficult for a single firm to master sufficient product knowledge, and this lack of specialization outweighs the benefits of bundling.

Even when obeying these two rules, global service may weaken the center. To avoid this, only develop global service if the customer explicitly desires it, and try to ensure synergy among products.

There are other instances where we can foresee a competitor's entry into a given segment that, although distinct from ours, nevertheless poses a threat. This might be by stealing some of our customers now, or by developing know-how in order to attack us in the future.

To deal with this scenario, we need different forms of defense. The first of these is the pre-emptive strike.

4.5 Pre-emptive strikes

There are two distinctive characteristics of pre-emptive strikes. First, there is entry into new markets, which differentiates it from defenses where no movement is involved. Second, the movement occurs before the competitor's move – so it is distinct from blocking or counter-attacks.

Pre-emptive strikes can be directed towards one of three segments. There is the segment the competitor is considering entering; the segment the competitor is in at the moment; and a segment where the competitor is not present, but where the segment is so similar that it threatens the segment the competitor is in. Figure 4.6 summarizes the major characteristics.

The motto of the pre-emptive strike is: attack is the best defense – especially if it is unexpected and sudden. The Iraq war in 2003[6] and Pearl Harbour in 1941 were pre-emptive strikes, predicated on political rationales.

It is also a strategy frequently practised in business. There can be product, client, need, or location pre-emptive strikes.

Federal Express (FedEx) conducted a successful *product* pre-emptive strike against Airborne Express. Following successful marketing tests of FedEx's new overnight express letter service in the late 1980s, Airborne conducted similar test markets in Cleveland, Philadelphia, and Hartford. Federal Express immediately entered Airborne's test markets with its own product, distorting Airborne's test results and attracting customers to FedEx's better-known brand.

American Broadcasting Corporation (ABC) achieved an impressive *client* pre-emptive strike against its CBS and NBC rivals with daytime TV serials and dramas aimed at women. Due to high viewer ratings, ABC could afford to set up a sales force specializing in selling daytime TV to advertisers. ABC

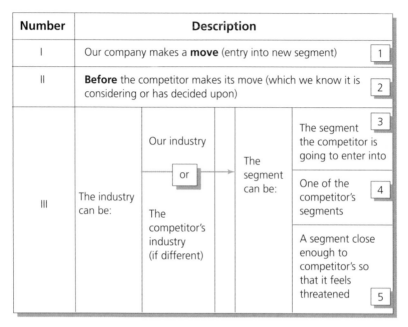

Number	Description
I	Our company makes a **move** (entry into new segment) `1`
II	**Before** the competitor makes its move (which we know it is considering or has decided upon) `2`
III	The industry can be: Our industry *or* The competitor's industry (if different) → The segment can be: The segment the competitor is going to enter into `3` One of the competitor's segments `4` A segment close enough to competitor's so that it feels threatened `5`

Figure 4.6 ◆ Characteristics of a pre-emptive strike

could also achieve lower production costs by paying its actors lower rates and shooting on inexpensive sets and locations. As a result of these efficiencies, ABC reached a commanding position and gained high returns. At one point, 25 percent of ABC's sales revenues and 40 percent of its profits were coming from the six daytime serials directed at housewives.

A *need* pre-emptive strike is illustrated by Thompson Medical, manufacturer of Slim-Fast, a diet powder drink. To prevent entry by competitors, Thompson decreased the price of Slim-Fast almost to cost level. It then launched Ultra Slim-Fast, which cost a lot more – directed at a wealthy market that was willing to pay a higher price for a better product. Thompson thus ensured that all doors to the market were closed.

Doktor Pet, a pet franchising chain, illustrates *location* pre-emptive strikes in terms of distribution.[7] It signed leases in 150 shopping malls in the USA, whether it had a franchisee lined up or not.

Not all pre-emptive strikes are successful. When Mastercard announced that it was launching travellers' cheques, Visa quickly upstaged Mastercard and launched its travellers' cheques first. However, five years later, none of the 13 banks issuing Visa travellers' cheques were making a profit.

Why not? Because Visa had underestimated the length of time that it would take for travellers' cheques to become profitable. The emergence of two companies in the market in such a short time created a price war that benefited the customer but no-one else, not even third-party agent banks selling their cheques. The lesson is that while pre-emptive strikes provide the defender with the initiative, they are short-term solutions to business conflict, unless the potential aggressor is completely forced out of the marketplace. Otherwise there will be a continuous challenge to the defender.

Therefore it is important that pre-emptive strikes are implemented well. There are three major conditions for success to be met. The first is a pre-requisite, the second facilitates success, and the third increases the expected return from the pre-emptive strike.

The pre-requisite is competitor intelligence. Japanese firms have achieved a number of intelligence coups in Silicon Valley through the systematic surveillance of published information, coupled with aggressive collection of competitor data using reverse engineering of products, extensive field interviews, the selective development of customer and supplier contacts, and facility site inspections.

Toyota has a broad-focussed intelligence system that provides it with systematic information about competitor's methods, organization, management, products, and technology.

Some American companies also use intelligence systems to great advantage. Gillette noted that Bic, which pioneered disposable razors in Europe in 1975, had introduced the disposable razor in Canada in early 1976. Gillette perceived that Bic was encroaching on the US market and was thus a major potential competitor. In response, Gillette rushed into manufacturing its Good News disposable razor on the national US market in early 1976. Bic followed with US test markets in mid-1976, but Gillette had already paved the way for its dominance of this market.

Second, the benefit of surprise facilitates the defense. Frederick the Great, King of Prussia, said that 'success lies most in what the enemy expects last'.

But to keep surprise on our side, we must involve few people in the decision, act fast when the decision has been made, and apply all our force (i.e. advertising, marketing, product improvements) at the same time. Indeed, the quicker we act, the easier it is to surprise. Von Clausewitz stressed that 'no battle can be concluded too fast'.

Firms should follow the example of the Romans. The moment they knew that conflict was inevitable they declared war, since any delay would be advantageous for the enemy. The objective was to avoid postponing the inevitable.

If the segment is small (or our entry so large that there is little room for anyone to follow suit), pre-emptive attacks are a good choice.

Chicago Business occupies a small segment – business specifically in Chicago. There is no room for a me-too magazine there. *Fifth Avenue* occupies a similar niche in New York, covering social events in Fifth Avenue. There is no point in a rival launching a second social calendar magazine focussing on that one block. If the segment is small enough, or if you enter large enough, you will discourage competitors from following suit.

And the fewer the number of firms already in the segment, the better. That will increase the likelihood of customers associating the segment with our brand. This helps explain why *Time* is ahead of *Newsweek*, *People* is ahead of *US*, *Playboy* outsells *Penthouse*, *TV Guide* outsells *Curtis*, and so on. Figure 4.7 summarizes how to implement pre-emptive strikes.

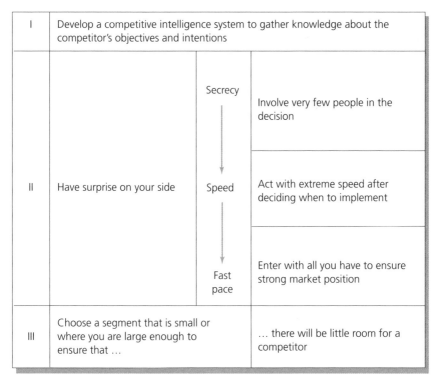

I	Develop a competitive intelligence system to gather knowledge about the competitor's objectives and intentions		
		Secrecy	Involve very few people in the decision
II	Have surprise on your side	Speed	Act with extreme speed after deciding when to implement
		Fast pace	Enter with all you have to ensure strong market position
III	Choose a segment that is small or where you are large enough to ensure that …		… there will be little room for a competitor

Figure 4.7 ◆ How to perform pre-emptive strikes

However, pre-emptive strikes have a major limitation: they require previous knowledge of a competitor's intentions. What happens when we don't have that knowledge? We can only react after the competitor has moved – by blocking or counter-attacking.

4.6 Blocking

Blocking entry is the fifth form of defense. It distinguishes itself from signaling and holding the ground because there is movement. It is different from pre-emptive strike, counter-attack, and strategic withdrawal since the movement is towards the segment the competitor has entered.

The essence of blocking is that, when a competitor enters into a given segment, where we are not present, we decide to respond by entering that segment too, in order to protect ourselves. The objective is to prevent a problem (a competitor's move into a specific segment) from becoming an emergency. Time, here, is part of the problem, not of the solution.

Frequently firms that fail to block the entry of a competitor come to regret it. IBM is a good example. When DEC introduced minicomputers, IBM had to decide if it would be competitive with the mainframe or not. Should IBM adapt its mainframes or ignore DEC's minicomputers? When IBM finally decided to launch a minicomputer of its own, DEC had had enough time to make fast progress without serious competition and become the second largest computer company in the world.

Wilson MacGregor, Spalding, and Karsten Manufacturing dominated golf club production until a few years ago. But to their regret they failed to block Callaway Golf Company, which introduced the first oversized driver, and Cobra Golf, which launched oversized irons. Leading ski manufacturers like Salomon, Rossignol, and Atomic failed to promptly block the introduction of the snowboard, from J. Burton's Snowboards Inc.

Another example is when traditional roller skate manufacturers didn't react promptly enough to rollerblades, which shook the whole industry up. Today, Rollerblade Inc., which pioneered the product, has almost 50 percent market share. These are all cases where failing to block entry created very serious problems for the market leader(s).

A successful entry blockage was carried out by British Airways. BA blocked four no-frills European carriers (Ryanair, easyJet, Debonair, and Virgin Express) by creating its own no-frills carrier, Go. Go benefited from BA's market dominance and the resources that BA was able to divert into it. However, the blockage was successful at a cost. It was such a drain on resources that eventually BA sold it, and the other no-frills companies have thrived. Stelios Haji-Ioannou, founder of easyJet, said at the time, 'It is impossible to compete against someone who is trying to lose money'.

As with every strategy, sometimes blocking fails. For example, when General Motors tried to block Mercedes and BMW by launching the Seville, the product was perceived as being inferior to both German manufacturers' cars.

4.6.2 Using blocking

Success or failure in blocking depends on four rules that must be followed:

◆ Act swiftly.

◆ Act boldly.

◆ Use a new name.

◆ Be sure you have competitive advantage.

Act swiftly so that the competitor does not have time to react. If we block later rather than sooner, the competitor will learn more about the segment and build market share. Hesitation is to be avoided. When Seven-Up aggressively promoted its caffeine-free cola product Like, Pepsi-Cola quickly formulated its own caffeine-free drink, Pepsi-Free, and promoted it with a strong advertising campaign.

Acting early must be reinforced by *acting boldly*. Avoid the Japanese work ethic 'kaizen' – incremental, continuous, but gradual improvement. While kaizen can perform wonders for manufacturing, it can be a disaster in strategy. In strategy, small improvements are likely to mean that the blockage will be insubstantial and reinforced too slowly, because it gives the competitor time to react.

'Many assume that half efforts can be effective', wrote Carl von Clausewitz. 'A small jump is easier than a large one, but no one wishing to cross a wide ditch would cross half of it first.' The lesson for business is that we must go after our competitor(s) with all we have got in terms of advertising, sales promotion, price benefits, model variations, etc. Throw all you have into the market arena to try to knock out the competitor, as fast as you can.

For example, to launch Acura, Honda set up a nationwide chain of dealers that was entirely separate from existing Honda dealerships. To launch Aleve, Procter & Gamble spent $60 million in advertising and another $40 million in sales promotion.

Third, give the new model a *new name*. Keep the corporation's name, but find a new brand name. For example, Bayer tried to launch acetaminophen as a 'non-aspirin' pain reliever. The product went nowhere. Names like Bayer, IBM, Hershey, and Wrigley provide an umbrella image of quality, but the new product needs something new to differentiate it.

Finally, we must have some kind of *competitive advantage*. This can either be synergy due to sharing of resources, or because we have greater strengths than competitors in the new segment that we are defending.

Encyclopedia Britannica failed to block Microsoft's CD-ROM encyclopedia *Encarta*. *Britannica* is a 32 volume collection of books, costing some $1500; *Encarta* is about $55. *Britannica* chose to concentrate on the material value offered by a set of impressive, beautifully bound books. The strategy failed and *Britannica* started to make losses. As a blocking strategy, *Britannica* brought out a CD-ROM version. But it still costs $995 and does not have the multimedia qualities of *Encarta*. The blocking strategy was too slow and too weak and *Britannica*'s sales are still decreasing.

Figure 4.8 summarizes the four principles for successful blockage.

How	Why
1 Move swiftly	To prevent the competitor strengthening its position
2 Move boldly	To maximize impact through force
3 Create a new brand name	To show customers that the new brand is distinct from the old one
4 Maximize synergy	To create competitive advantage
5 Be sure your strengths are equal to the new segment's success factors	

Figure 4.8 ◆ Successful blocking techniques

But what if we have let too much time go by? Or we cannot put enough resources together to cross the trench in strength? Or we are unable to find an appropriate name? Or we lack competitive advantage?

Then we should skip blocking and attack a segment different from the one the competitor has entered. This is called counter-attack, which we consider next.

4.7 Counter-attack

Churchill used to say, 'to every blow struck in war there is a counter'. This is the essence of a counter-attack. The adversary attacks and we in turn defend ourselves by attacking.

Counter-attacking is distinct from blocking since it means entry into a different segment from that which the competitor has attacked in. That segment can be one in which the competitor is present or absent – as long as our presence there threatens the competitor.

So there are three types of counter-attack. The first – *counter-attacking the competitor's original segment*, is demonstrated by Mercedes. BMW introduced more expensive models (Series 5, 7 and 8) in order to challenge Mercedes head-on, so Mercedes counter-attacked by introducing less expensive models (Series 190, later called C), which fought directly with BMW's original models (Series 3). BMW upgraded, Mercedes downgraded. Attack and counter-attack.

An example of counter-attacks into *new segments* is provided by the Swiss watch industry. In the 1980s the major brands (ertina, Longines, Tissot, and Rado) saw their world market share fall to 8 percent from 30 percent a decade earlier. They lost two segments: electronic/digital and low cost. Japanese brands Casio, Citizen, and Seiko overtook in these segments.

The Swiss companies began a belated counter-attack as the Japanese brands started to move into the higher quality, high margin products that were the backbone of the Swiss watch industry. The Swiss counter-attack was based on a new product characterized by electronic quartz technology, low cost, and fashion. Swatch used industrial robots to cut production costs, a variety of colors to match fashion, and a hardened resin case to resist shock and temperature changes.

An example of the third type – counter-attacking *in two different industries* – is IBM's retaliation to Xerox's entry into the mainframe computer market. While Xerox's XDS computer division was locked in an all-out frontal attack on IBM, IBM launched photocopying machines targeted right at the heart of Xerox's line of products. Xerox, faced with a two front war of attrition, was forced to sell its XDS division to Honeywell after several years of losses.

Counter-attacks generally have three important qualities. First, they can involve one or several segments. Pressed by Campbell's Soup and Hunt, Cheeseborough-Ponds entered not one but four sauce segments: meat, salads, pizza, and spaghetti.

Second, a counter-attack can be performed alone or together with other strategies. When Wolfschmidt attacked Smirnoff Vodka, claiming equal quality at $1 cheaper, Smirnoff followed several strategies: two counter-attacks and one blockage. The counter-attacks positioned Smirnoff in a higher price segment and launched another brand, Popov, for the lower-priced market, costing even less than Wolfschmidt's. And then Smirnoff blocked Wolfschmidt's entry with a newly created and equally priced brand: Reskla.

Third, the objective of a counter-attack is not to harvest the profit potential of the segment(s) we enter, but to weaken the competitor in its new segment.

So we may ask, why not simply block the competitor's entry into that segment? Because we can do more harm to the competitor by entering into another segment.

4.7.1 How to perform a counter-attack

The segment where the counter-attack is performed must preferably have several characteristics. It should represent a large percentage of the competitor's sales, or have a high crossover with the competitor's segment, and be synergistic with other segments the competitor is in, thus indicating to the competitor that we might enter there too.

We still need competitive advantage as well as the these three characteristics though, to show that we have the capability to put the theory into practice.

Tic Tac was able to gain a 12 percent market share of the hard candy and mint category within a few years. However, then it was attacked by Life Savers, Warner Lambert's Dynamints, and German's Ragold, which copied Tic Tac's clean plastic packaging and positioned themselves as sugar-free. Subsequently, Tic Tac's market share dropped to 2 percent.

Tic Tac counter-attacked by creating a distinction between sugar-free and calorie-free. Since Tic Tacs had the lowest amount of calories of all the competiting products, and Americans are very calorie conscious, Tic Tac repositioned its brand for this segment, using the slogan 'Tic Tac the 1½ calorie breath mint'. As a consequence, its market share returned to almost 12 percent.

What if we lack a competitive advantage to perform a counter-attack? The option left is holding the ground, i.e. stay put and prepare to engage the competitor when or if it decides to enter the segment(s) we are presently in.

4.8 Holding the ground

We have seen six strategies already. Three of them (signaling, entry barriers, and global service) are intent on dissuasion – keeping competition out. Three more (pre-emptive strike, blockage, and counter-attack) involve movement – entry into segments other than those we are presently in.

Now we turn to a different type of strategy: we stay put in our present segments, a competitor enters them, and we fight it out. Holding the ground represents engagement in our present segments. But what do we use to make a stand?

The answer is with the functional areas of the business: marketing (advertising, sales promotion, pricing, channels of distribution, etc.); manufacturing (lowering costs, faster delivery, using robots to increase flexibility, etc.); accounting (better and faster controls); finance (better purchase conditions); human resources (higher motivation, better selection, and training); information systems management; the administrative area (building and equipment conservation, communications); the general management area (the organization chart; controls; co-ordination mechanisms); and the degree of centralization.

Holding the ground is about tactics. The strategic decision was to stay put. Tactics will then decide the outcome of the battle.[8] Consider cost reduction to strengthen competitiveness. Nippon Steel developed a company-wide campaign to reduce cost. As a consequence, production processes were improved to reduce labor requirements and substantial investments were made in energy-efficient and labor-saving facilities. These included continuous casters, blast-furnaces, and new equipment combining intermittent operations with continuous operations. All this upgraded the quality of Nippon products as well as developing new products in order to maintain its competitive position throughout the world.

Marketing is another competitive weapon. When Kodak faced a major challenge from Fuji to its leading position in the US film market, it used a combination of price cuts and a major advertising campaign to encourage customers to ask for Kodak paper by name. This was assisted by better support services for photofinishers, including a sophisticated computer-aided fault diagnosis service.

Finance can also play a role. Xerox used it as a weapon in its photocopier business. By leasing rather than selling photocopiers, Xerox forced its early competitors to either fund the large amounts of working capital necessary for a large-scale leasing operation or leave the market.

There are two things worth noting about innovation. First, the changes in the product or value chain must be hard to replicate. Otherwise copy by competitors will rapidly erode the previous competitive advantage. Second, whatever the tactical weapons used, it can be carried out autonomously or with the help of an alliance.

To fight off Japanese competition from the European video-recorder market, Philips made an alliance with German manufacturer Grundig to create a strong European distribution network. To obtain a competitive advantage over Japanese firms, many US companies have established joint programmes in product and process R&D in semi-conductors and computers. Micro Electronics, Computer Technology Corporation, and Semiconductor Research Corporation are such examples. The aims vary from studying artificial intelligence to developing new computer design or computer-aided manufacturing tools (CAM) for the future production of very large-scale integrated chips.

4.8.1 How to hold the ground

Regardless of the tactics used in marketing, manufacturing, etc., the outcome will depend on four issues: size; strengths (quality of resources); experience; and synergy.

Size

As seen in Chapter 3, size matters. Bic used its financial muscle to absorb several years of heavy losses incurred by low pricing and intensive advertising of its disposable ballpoint pens, lighters, and razors. It priced them low to penetrate the market and build a large market share, which brought future profits through volume. The idea that the winner in market share will face lower losses in profits in the first years than the loser is simply not true.[9]

In other words, if confronting forces are not proportional, winning the battle may not be enough – it will be a Pyrrhic victory.[10]

Quality of resources

In each segment, those firms with better quality in success factors (whether they be location, process, R&D, image, etc.) will outperform competition. Porsche has kept its prominence in the high-end sports cars segment through excellence in status, engine performance, and specification – Porsche offers multiple combinations of accessories down to the shape of the lights and the type of seats, enabling each Porsche to be truly unique – if the client is willing to pay for it.

Experience

The higher the cumulative volume of production achieved since day one, the lower the costs. This creates the possibility of lowering prices and enticing customers away from the competition. The rate at which cumulative production decreases costs varies from market to market, but it can be considerable: in 1958, Toyota was producing 1.5 cars per employee per year. By 1965, the ratio had increased to 1:23, and by 1969 it was 1:39. See Chapter 7 for a case study on the Japanese car industry.

Synergy

It will be beneficial if the segment under attack benefits from resource sharing with other segments. Our strength in other segments can then influence the outcome of the struggle.

Synergy exploits similarities between such products as magazines and motion pictures (Time Warner), consumer electronics and motion pictures (Sony's acquisition of Columbia), cable and telephone (NCR). Synergy can also exist between more than two industries: photolithography, cameras and copiers (Canon);[11] calculators, TV screens, watches, and musical instruments (Casio);[12] motorcycles, cars, lawn mowers, and power generation equipment (Honda);[13] and PBXs, hybrid analogue-digital switches and fully configured office switches (Northern Telecom).[14]

But whatever the source and how many industries involved in the synergy, real benefits depend on the degree of similarity or convergence between industries and the internal organization of a company to exploit them. Central departments serving various SBUs, transference of managers, and top management units providing inputs to several businesses, for example.

What if our competitor is better off when we balance these four factors?

We have two options. If the difference is small enough and the segment attractive enough for our company to remain profitable, we can stay in that segment – although we will no longer be leaders.

If that is not the case, staying in the segment will mean losses.[15] In such a case, we will be better off if we withdraw – the last resort strategy.

4.9 Withdrawal

This is the last defensive strategy. It is a defense with negative movement. It increases market distance from a competitor, but is not the same as giving up. It is sacrifice rather than surrender.

A company withdraws to attack strongly in a different direction. Why? Because resources are scarce. 'He who defends everything, defends nothing' (Ferdinand Foch). After all, 'the essence of strategy is to apply scarce resources to the greatest opportunities' (Peter F. Drucker).

Withdrawal is the strategy by which we accept losing a battle so that we still have a chance to win the war, instead of wasting time and resources in a hopeless situation. 'Victory goes to he who knows when to fight, and when not to' (Sun Tzu).

Philip Morris introduced Marlboro in 1937 as a cigarette for women. 'Ivory tip, protect the lip' and 'Mild as May' were the advertisement slogans. Almost two decades later the brand had less than 0.1 percent of the market. In 1954 Philip Morris decided to perform a sex change on Marlboro. From now on the brand would be for men. The advertisements featured a masculine, virile cowboy. In the first year of the new campaign Marlboro brand captured 2 percent of the market. It steadily increased its share until in 1976 it beat Winston to become the largest selling cigarette brand in the USA.

Bell Sport manufactured both motorcycle and bicycle helmets. It was never able to achieve a leading position in either market. Then in 1991 Bell dropped motorcycle helmets and moved full-time into bicycle helmets. Sales, profits, and market share went up substantially, reaching 50 percent of the market in the mid-1990s.

These two examples show withdrawals from one segment to another, within the same industry. But withdrawals are not limited to segments – Sinclair withdrew from an entire industry when it abandoned the digital watch market because of competitors' aggressive pricing and intensive product development. Withdrawal can also be geographical, as when Coca-Cola and IBM withdrew from India to avoid the requirement of transfer of technology to local firms.

Sometimes withdrawals are from both a geographic area and from an industry: Cable & Wireless announced that it would pull out of the USA in June 2003. Three months before, it withdrew from the cable TV industry.

Failures in withdrawal can be due to implementation (the 'how' was badly managed) or to a wrong strategic decision: either the segment one withdraws to is not a good choice, or the company should not have withdrawn at all (the 'when' was mismanaged).

Braniff International Airlines went bankrupt as a result of a series of disastrous moves. It abandoned unprofitable routes, but instead of introducing a few carefully selected new ones, it launched a myriad of routes to US cities, Europe and Latin America. Then Braniff was unable to keep operating costs down because there was a mismatch between its portfolio of aircrafts and the routes it flew.

In addition, withdrawal errors frequently occur when companies, not content with the low margins at the low end of an industry, decide to concentrate on the high end. That creates a window of opportunity for competitors to occupy the low end of the market, generate money, solidify their relations with suppliers, distributors and clients, improve their image, and then have a stronger position to move up the market.

This is how many Japanese companies arrived at their luxury brand: Nissan's Infinity, Toyota's Lexus, Honda's Acura. Sony started as a manufacturer of private labels for retail chains, then introduced the Tummy TV, then a slightly higher-priced model, and so on.

It is important to know when and how to withdraw. This will be analyzed in Chapter 5, which discusses *when* each strategy should be adopted.

If the product is a dog, the company should consider dropping it. However, the important thing to stress here is that a product does not have to be a dog before the company should consider withdrawing it.

Two rules have been developed to indicate when to withdraw. The most aggressive was put forward by Jack Welch, former CEO of General Electric. 'All companies which are not number one or number two in their business, should be divested.' Welch thought that 'companies should search out and participate in the real growth industries and insist upon being number one or number two in every business they are in. Management and companies that don't do this and hang on to losers, won't be around for long.'

Less severe is the rule that allows a company to be lower than number two in the business as long as at least one of two things happen: the company must still be higher than the average competition in terms of quality on the success factor list; and/or the business the company is in is very attractive (in terms of growth, volume and margin). Divestment will then not be necessary, as long as the cost of capital is included in the calculations.

Whatever the rule one follows to decide when to divest, implementation should follow several guidelines.

First, one must decide if withdrawal must be *total* or only *partial*. We can abandon all of our present segments or just a few. The decision depends on three factors: how attractive (in sales volume, rate of growth and margin) our segments are; how strong our competitive position is (do our strengths match the segments key success factors?); and how important synergy is in this segment and others we are in.

Home Furniture Store used to sell a complete range of furniture: all types for office and home. Under pressure from new entrants such as Levitz, Home decided to abandon everything except two segments: chairs and sofas. This is a partial withdrawal. But when Interstate Department Stores went bankrupt, it dropped all its products, abandoned the discount market, and moved into toys under a new name: Toys R Us.

Having decided to withdraw, consider as a first option entering a niche within our segment. Under pressure from other women's magazines, Lear's chose to concentrate on the mature niche. The advantages are twofold: greater focus and a withdrawal to charted territory.

If we cannot find a suitable niche within our segment to withdraw to, we should look for other segments close to ours. The chances are that the new segment's success factors will be similar to those of our previous segments. SAS (Scandinavian Airlines System) withdrew from the economy class into business class (the executive segment). Not to a different aviation segment like merchandise transportation, nor to another industry.

If neither niches nor close segments can be found, one should look for other segments in our industry before considering moving into another industry. Back in 1985, Intel made a strategic shift from memory chips to microprocessors, a market in which the company now has a large market share.

There is then the issue of how to organize the withdrawal (see Figure 4.9). There are basically three ways: exchange for another division of another company; sell the division; or close it outright. What to do depends upon whether there is another company interested in our division, and if that company has a business we are interested in.

If another company is interested and also has a business we are interested in, we can swap divisions – this is the easiest and fastest way to withdraw. General Electric did this several times. 'Thomson, France's government-owned electronics company had a very weak medical imaging business called CGR that I wanted,' Jack Welch relates. 'I decided to see if he might be interested in a trade . . . I began to write down businesses we could swap for their medical operations . . . I tried the TV manufacturing business. He liked the idea immediately. Alain (Thompson's chairman) saw the trade as a way to

From where	1 Total or partial withdrawal
Where to	2 Niche within segment
	3 Close segment within the same industry
	4 Other segment within the same industry
	5 Other industry
How to organize it	6 Exchange for another division of another company
	7 Sell the division
	8 Close it

How fast

What is → The chance the competitor will follow us into other segments? / Our loss in relation to that of our competitors? ↓	Low	High
Higher (ours)	2 Fast	1 Fastest
Lower (ours)	3 Slow	4 Slowest

The businesses left in the portfolio	Must constitute a coherent set	Without cannibalization and If possible, benefit from synergy

Figure 4.9 ◆ How to withdraw

become the number one producer of TV sets in the world overnight (his TV business was subscale and strictly Europe based)'.

How quickly should we withdraw? Once the decision has been made, the general rule is that one should implement it as fast as possible. Time is money and we are losing both in the segment we are planning to withdraw from.

There are two conditions which, if they occur together, make an exception to the rule. First, when we are certain that the competitor plans to follow us into the segment we are withdrawing to (because the segment is very attractive and/or synergetic with the competitor's markets). Second, when, due to our presence in the segment we are going to withdraw from, the competitor is proportionally losing more money than we are. Unless these conditions are met, the sooner we implement our divestment decision, the better.

Finally it is important to make sure that our remaining businesses constitute a coherent set. They must have synergy with each other.

In the 1980s GM decided to focus on the middle market segments because of pressure from Japan and Germany. But it did so without clearly distinguishing its models which were frequently similar in characteristics and overlapped in price ranges. Rather than generate support, cohesion and synergy, GM's decision led to cannibalism, compounding GM's difficulties.

Withdrawal is not the end – it can be a new beginning, if it is properly managed.

4.10 Summary

First, one can distinguish among defense strategies in terms of timing. If we defend before the competitor attacks, there are four types we can use.

1 Signalling.

2 Creating entry barriers (fixed or mobile).

3 Global service.

4 Pre-emptive strikes.

Blockage and counter-attacks take place simultaneously with the competitor's move. Holding the ground and withdrawal occur after the competitor has made its move.

Then defense strategies differ depending on whether our attention is directed towards the competitor's original segment(s); the segment the competitor enters; or none of the above.

Figure 4.10 shows how to categorize the eight types of defense strategy we have analysed in this chapter.

These eight strategies, together with the six types of attack strategies, form a total of fourteen possible strategic movements. We have seen the characteristics of each and how to implement them. But the question remains: when should we attack or defend?

That leads us to the major question of *timing*.

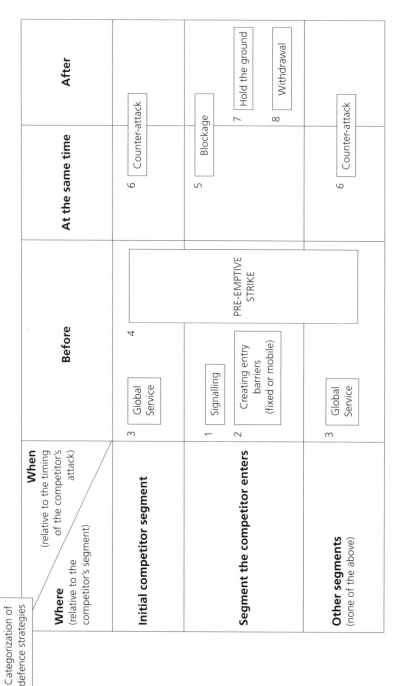

Figure 4.10 ◆ The eight defense strategies

5

When to follow each strategic movement

"The defensive form of war is in itself stronger than the offence."

Carl von Clausewitz

5.1 Introduction

IN BUSINESS AND IN LIFE, we must know when to attack and when not to. When to stand still, and when to withdraw.

The strategist must follow three main principles. First, defense is easier than attack. So, when in doubt do not attack. Defense must receive the benefit of the doubt; attack the burden of proof. The reasons are discussed in Section 5.2.

If we opt for defense, we must still decide which strategy to adopt. Section 5.3 shows how to choose.

If we decide to attack, we have to choose the type of attack. Section 5.4 shows when each choice should be made.

5.2 Choosing between attack and defense

It is well known that defending your markets is easier than attacking new ones. A survey by Bain & Co. of more than 2000 companies in a variety of industries (technology, service, and product) concluded that 'the major reason why many businesses fail to deliver value to customers and shareholders is that they wander too far from their core businesses, where the bulk of their strengths lie'.

Diversification from the core can actually destroy the value a company promises and severely limit the amount and breadth of possible profitable growth.[1]

Why is defense better than attack? There are six reasons:

◆ The company may have first move advantage.

◆ Knowledge of the industry.

◆ Experience (learning curve).

◆ Market share.

◆ Scale advantages.

◆ Client's risk aversion.

These six qualities have all been defined earlier in this book.

A survey of 25 leading brands in 1923[2] shows why first move advantage and the customers' reticence to switch to a new brand is so relevant. Sixty years after the survey, 20 of the brands were still number one in their markets. Four had fallen to second place. One was in fifth place.

The lesson? It is difficult, although not impossible, to dethrone a king. So why do so many companies opt for attack? There are three reasons. First, managers get bored with the same old stuff. Second, attacks gain media attention. And third, the newness of an attack creates a sense of heroism. This is why in spite of the six disadvantages of attack, business pages are full of examples of 'Charges of the Light Brigade'.

In order to avoid blunders, a company should attack only if three conditions are met:

1   All the criteria described in Chapter 3 are met.

2   The attack does not create risk by weakening our center.

3   There is less to gain from increasing market share than from entering new market segments. This might be because, by having too low a share, we are too feeble to attack the dominant competitors. Or it might be that even if we have the largest share, it is increasingly difficult to attract new customers because they are loyal to other brands or are non-category users. The diagram below illustrates this.

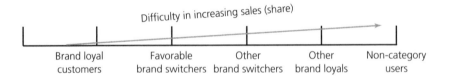

There are four criteria to consider before launching an attack:

1   Have we organized our defense (through entry barriers, signaling, etc.) in such a way that the threat of a new entrant is negligible?[3] (Two or three years is usually an adequate time span.)

2   Are we sure we can spare the resources for the attack, and that by doing so we won't endanger our present market share position?

3   Is it more attractive, dollar for dollar, to invest in the new segments than in increasing the share in the old one?

4   Is there a type of attack that satisfies all the required criteria in Chapter 3?

If the answer to all these four questions is yes, then we should go ahead with the planned attack.

However, imagine a situation where there is a 25% chance that a competitor will enter in the next two or three years. We estimate that 25% of the resources diverted into a new venture could be used to maintain our present market share position. (Thus, 75% of the resources will not be missed.) Also, there is a 50% chance that the new segment will be more attractive[4] than the average of the present ones. And finally, we believe that a guerrilla attack stands the most chance of success, but we can only be sure of meeting six of its nine required criteria for success. That is a 66% chance.

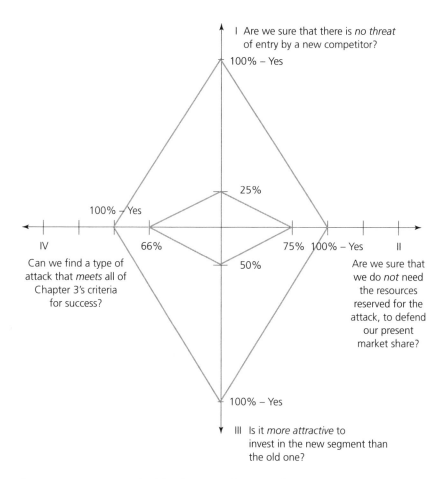

Figure 5.1 ◆ How to decide if an attack is justified by the odds

In such a case, instead of being 100% sure that we should go ahead with the attack, our assurance is 25%, 75%, 50% and 66%. Adding it all up it comes to 216%, which over the maximum possible of 400% (4 × 100%) is 58%.

In such a situation an attack is clearly risky. The attack should not be implemented, and the company should opt for defense.

As a rule of thumb, for an attack to be successful it should have odds of at least two to one – that is, a total score of at least 66% × 4 = 264%.

Figure 5.1 shows this concept diagrammatically. Companies in the outer lozenge should go ahead with the planned attack. Companies in the inner situation should not. Other situations will fall in between. In Figure 5.1 the outer lozenge corresponds to the first example, i.e. 100% positive in all answers. The inner lozenge refers to the second example, i.e. 25%, 75%, 50% and 66% chances of success.

5.3 When to choose a defense strategy

How can we decide when to follow each defense strategy? First, check which strategy satisfies its required implementation criteria, as indicated in the previous chapter. This suggestion has an inherent fault, however, because if there are two or more strategies whose implementation criteria are met, not all strategies are equally advisable in all circumstances.

However, there are steps we can take to help us decide. On the whole, if the implementation criteria are met, follow the first three strategies – signaling, creating entry barriers, and globalizing service. The remaining five strategies are advisable only in certain circumstances.

If the competitor has already firmly decided to enter our segment, it is best to create a surprise – through blocking, counter-attack, pre-emptive strike, or holding the ground. The first two strategies are purely defensive. The second two involve an attack, but provoked by competition, and so count as defense not attack.

Our belief that defense is stronger than attack gives us some criteria for choosing between the last two defenses, holding the ground and withdrawing. First, we should ask if our company is competitive compared with the new entrant? If the answer to this question is 'no', then we should ask if our segment is still worth pursuing as a source of both sales 'margin, volume, and growth', and synergy (cost sharing with other business units: sales force, distribution, warehousing, etc.)?

Whatever the answer to the first question, if the answer to the second question is 'yes', the firm should hold its ground. If, however, the answer to *both* questions is 'no', then the company should withdraw. Figure 5.2 summarizes this analysis.

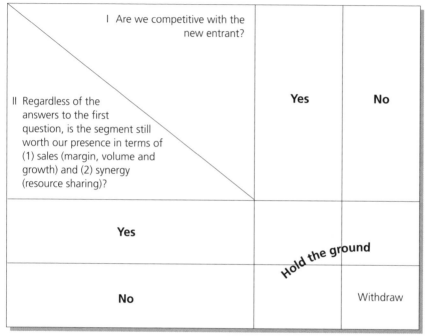

Figure 5.2 ◆ When to hold the ground and when to withdraw

If we opt for holding the ground, there is a third question to ask: Can we find a segment other than the one that we are in, where our entry will meet the following requirements:

◆ Will it seriously harm the competitor (threatening its market share, or pulling away its clients)?

◆ Will it harm the competitor more than if we simply applied those resources to holding our ground?

◆ Do we have the required resources?

If the answer to all three questions is 'yes', then a counter-attack or a preemptive strike should be performed. It can be a pre-emptive strike if we have

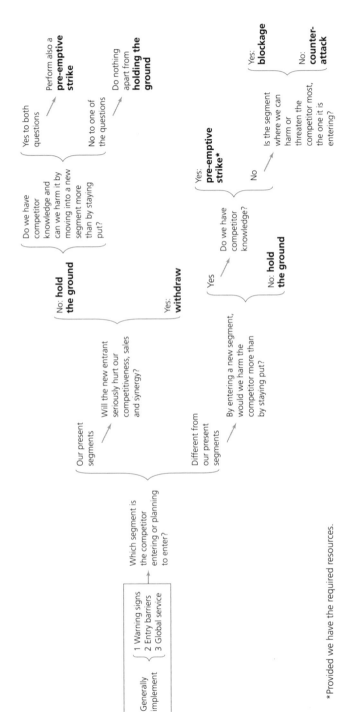

*Provided we have the required resources.

Figure 5.3 ◆ Which defense strategy to follow?

previous knowledge of the competitor's intentions, but will need to be a counter-attack if we do not.

The target segment can be one the competitor is in already, or sufficiently similar to be perceived as harmful to the competitor.

What if the competitor is planning to, or does indeed, enter a segment we are not present in, but still damages our sales or threatens to do so?

Three major strategic alternatives exist: pre-emptive strike, blocking, and counter-attack. The question is: Should we do any of them at all? The answer is 'yes', if again three requirements are met:

◆ The strategic move will seriously harm the competitor.

◆ We can act without weakening our center.

◆ We have the required resources.

Which of the three strategies should we follow? It comes down to two circumstances: if we have competitor knowledge, and which segment will harm the competitor most.

If the answer to any of the three questions above is 'no', then our company should not act but hold the ground. Figure 5.3 summarizes this reasoning.

If the competitor enters into one of our present segments, we should hold the ground if its entry does not considerably affect our competitiveness. However, if it does, we should withdraw.

Let us now suppose that our defensive situation is stable and our market position is safe. There is no threat from new entrants, and increasing market share in our present segments is not a productive option in terms of the ratio of potential benefits over required resources. We also have surplus resources that can productively be applied in other segments. If a firm meets all these criteria, then it can consider an attack. But which type?

5.4 When to choose an attack strategy

First, all the implementation criteria proposed in Chapter 3 for each strategy type must be met.

But what if both a bypass and an undifferentiated circle meet their implementation criteria? Which strategy should we then opt for? The answer is given by the likelihood of success of each strategy. From most likely to succeed to least likely, the order is:

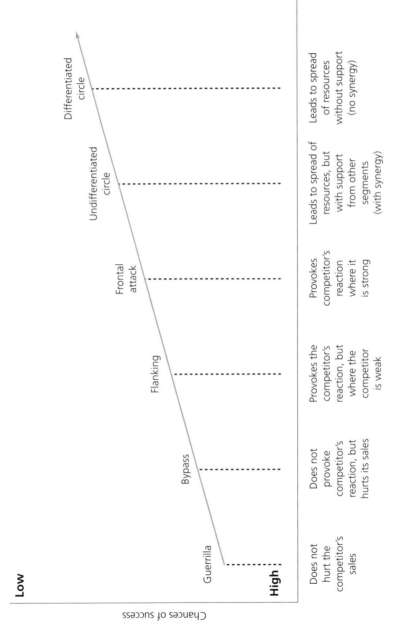

Figure 5.4 ◆ **Degrees of difficulty for attack strategies**

1 Guerrilla.

2 Bypass.

3 Flanking.

4 Frontal attack.

5 Undifferentiated circle.

6 Differentiated circle.

Chapter 3 explains why some strategies are more likely to succeed than others. Some strategies provoke the competitors, others do not. Guerrilla attacks provoke less than a bypass. A frontal attack is dangerous because the competitor can engage with us using its strengths, rather than its weaknesses.

Some strategies enable us to focus, while others require us to use lots of resources. That is the case with both undifferentiated and differentiated circles, which mean entry into more than one segment at a time. The other four attack strategies are more likely to succeed because they involve entry into one segment at a time.

Based on these criteria, guerrilla is the easiest and the differentiated circle the most difficult of the strategies. Other strategies fall in between, as shown in Figure 5.4. The easier a strategy, the greater the probability of success, all other things being equal, i.e. providing the required implementation criteria of each strategy are met equally (see Sections 3.2 to 3.7 in Chapter 3).

5.5 Conclusion

This chapter has presented a contingency theory for the eight defense and six attack strategies.

Three major principles were presented. First, defense is stronger than attack. An attack should be performed only when four criteria are met:

1 The new segments are more attractive than present ones.

2 There is no threat of potential entrants into our present segments.

3 The resources to be deployed in the attack are not necessary to defend our share position in our present markets.

4 We can find a type of attack that meets its success requirements (see Sections 3.2 to 3.7 in Chapter 3).

If most of these are not met, the company should choose a defense strategy. Situations in between should be managed as indicated in Section 5.2 and illustrated in Figure 5.1.

Not all strategies should be applied equally in all circumstances. Generally, all of the first three strategies should be followed – signaling, entry barriers, and global service. Choosing between holding the ground or withdrawing depends upon how the new entrant affects the company's competitiveness and consequently its sales (margin, volume, and growth) and synergy levels.

A blockage, counter-attack, or pre-emptive strike should be performed only if (1) it does not weaken the center; (2) serious harm is inflicted on the competitor; and (3) it is more productive, dollar for dollar, than investing in a greater share in our present markets.

Which of the three strategies to follow depends upon *when* one gets the information and *which segment* satisfies the above three criteria best.

If an attack is possible then priority should be given to a guerrilla strategy, followed by bypass, then flanking movement, then frontal attack, then undifferentiated circle, and, finally, differentiated circle.

6

Organizational alliances

"I alone against my brother;
I and my brother against my cousin;
I, my brother and my cousin, against my family;
I and my family against my village;
I and my village against the foreigner."

Arab Proverb

"The problem with alliances is that allies have opinions . . ."

Winston Churchill

6.1 Introduction

This chapter analyzes the role of organizational alliances in implementing the six types of attack and the eight types of defense. We shall divide the analysis into three elements: first, we need to recognize that there are 13 distinct types of organizational alliances; second, we'll look at the general advantages and disadvantages of alliances; and third, besides the general characteristics of all alliances, there is also a specific contribution made by each type. Depending on the specific situation, one or another type of alliance should be used. Section 6.5 offers questions that help to decide whether or not to make an alliance, and which type of alliance to opt for.

6.2 Thirteen types of alliances

The term 'organizational alliances' is a broad one that encompasses various types of association. The impact an alliance has can be minimal, as in an agreement on the technical specifications of the products bought and sold among organizations, or it can have a high impact, as when two firms opt for a merger (see Figure 6.1). Usually, as the impact increases, so does the durability of the alliance.

Figure 6.1(b) shows how durability and impact vary from a minimum in protocols[1] to a maximum in mergers. In between there are much used alliances such as consortiums (which are temporary joint ventures), private brand agreements (where a company markets a product manufactured by someone else under its own name), commercial agreements (when marketing is done under the manufacturer's name), dual marketing (where marketing is in the hands of a third party), the vendor–buyer agreement (which concerns product parts or components and not the commercial side), licensing (where a product patented by another company is licensed in return for royalties), and franchise.

In *franchising*, a local agent is responsible for the day-to-day running of the company – management and investment in premises. In return the franchise receives the benefits of the brand image, the company's knowledge and training, coaching, promotion, and procurement centralization (which creates benefits of experience and scale). This establishes service and operational standards. It teaches the secrets of the business, in exchange for royalties.

(a)

> 1 Protocols (agreements on the standard characteristics of the products, etc.)
> 2 Exchange of members of the board of directors
> 3 Consortiums
> 4 Private brand agreement
> 5 Dual marketing
> 6 Vendor/buyer agreement
> 7 Commercial agreement
> 8 Franchise
> 9 Licensing
> 10 Joint venture
> 11 Exchange of minority holdings
> 12 Acquisition
> 13 Merger
>
> (**Impact** and **duration** range from a minimum in 1, to a maximum in 13)

(b)

Durability / Impact	Low	High
Low		13 Merger 12 Acquisition 11 Exchange of minority holdings 10 Joint venture 9 Licensing 8 Franchise
High		7 Commercial agreement 6 Vendor/buyer agreement 5 Dual marketing 4 Private brand agreement 3 Consortiums 2 Exchange of members of the board of directors (exchange of board members) 1 Protocols (agreements on the standard characteristics of the products)

Figure 6.1 ◆ The thirteen types of association

Licensing is a manufacturing contract under which a product is designed and developed by one party, and manufactured by another. The first party benefits from saving on investment and is a security against a competitor manufacturing the product more cheaply and to a better degree of quality. The second party obtains access to proven technology.

In a *joint venture*, two or more parties set up a third one, but on a more permanent basis than in a consortium. Each party brings to the venture its own special skills, which should be different, relevant, and complementary to each other.

A *merger* differs from an acquisition, since both companies apparently disappear and a new, third company appears in its place.

6.3 Advantages and disadvantages of alliances

Alliances can be defensive or offensive. They can be tactical, where the company's market segments remain the same, or strategic, where there is an alteration in the company's market segments. Alliances can buy *time* and/or *strength* (*see* Figure 6.2).

Buying time is critical when there is a first move advantage into a new segment, and/or there is the need to occupy a market that has been enlarged due to globalization, or when diverting resources quickly will increase the chances of success. Many of the mergers of the 1990s were as a consequence of the perceived need to move rapidly into the new markets that appeared with the creation and expansion of economic blocks (APEC, European Union, Mercosur, NAFTA), and the increasing liberalization of trade among those economic blocks and deregulation.

Daimler-Benz's acquisition of Chrysler created the second largest world automotive company after Toyota, and enabled Daimler to expand rapidly across borders and into new market segments. Daimler had been trying for some years to launch subcompact models, and Chrysler's acquisition gave it a full portfolio of mass market cars and minivans.

Alliances can also buy skills, to do the same thing more effectively or do something new. The merger between Union des Banques Suisses (UBS) and Société des Banques Suisses (SBS) is a good example.

By merging their operations they planned to lay off 13,000 workers from a workforce of 56,000. The 23 percent saving in labor costs was supplemented by savings in other areas: closing redundant agencies and selling their real estate, for example.

The merger between Glaxo and Smithkline allowed for a 9 percent labor force reduction: 10,000 employees from a workforce of 112,000 were laid off, research facilities were shut down, and distribution and sales forces were

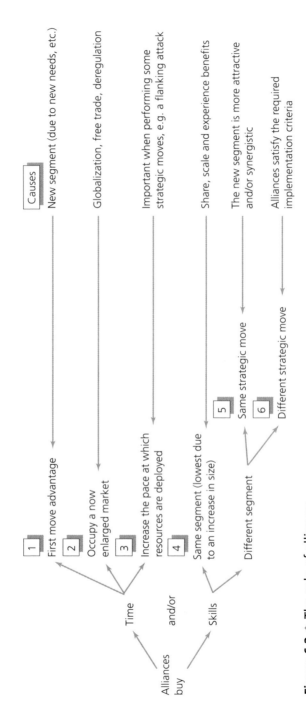

Figure 6.2 ◆ The role of alliances

reduced. Finally, the two companies' product portfolios complemented each other, enabling better customer service.

Alliances can also increase effectiveness (doing the right things), instead of efficiency (doing things right) when entering new market segments, as opposed to strengthening the company's position in present ones.

Greater effectiveness can be achieved either by implementing the same type of strategy in a more attractive segment, or by performing a different type of strategy altogether.[2]

Blue Bell, which manufactures Wrangler Jeans, provides an example of how alliances can allow for a strategic change. Here the change is in terms of geography and segment.

Blue Bell acquired Jantzen, a producer of swimwear, sweaters, shirts, blouses, and dresses. Jantzen, located on the west coast of the USA, offered the opportunity for Blue Bell to increase distribution of its existing products on the coast where it was weak in comparison to Levi's. Blue Bell's strength was in discount stores. So Jantzen also offered Blue Bell the opportunity to move into the mid-priced market favored by speciality and department stores.

Figure 6.2 summarizes the advantages of alliances: to buy time in terms of (1) first move advantage; (2) speed in occupying an enlarged market; (3) implementing the present strategy at a faster pace; (4) achieving greater efficiency due to increased share, scale and experience benefits; (5) entering more attractive and synergetic segments; and (6) implementing different strategic moves.

However, many alliances fail.[3] A failed alliance often happens because the wrong strategy was selected, or because of problems that arose because of the alliance itself and not because the strategy was wrong.

Why do so many alliances – e.g. Disney's takeover of Capital Cities, ABC, Allianz and Paribas Swedish Pharmacia and Upjohn – fail? Because an alliance involves compromise and a new working philosophy. These two problems sometimes outweigh the benefits, for five reasons.

The first reason is *lack of synergy*. The SPX acquisition of General Signal Corporation is a good example. SPX is a long-established producer of parts for car manufacturers, diagnostic equipment, and specialized tools for franchised dealers and independent repair shops. General Signal consisted of 15 separate businesses, only one of which dealt with cars. The others manufactured pumps, electronic controls, power systems, and radio frequency transmission systems. Consequently, there was little synergy between General Signal and SPX.

So the first reason why alliances may fail is that they have a low potential at start-up.

Another reason is that alliances can be *costly*. They can require a compromise – sharing of sales and profits. In acquisitions, sometimes an excessive premium is paid. In franchises and licenses, royalties can be excessive. As the old adage says, what is negotiated is what one gets. And this is not always greater than what was given away: sometimes the potential gains to be harvested from greater share scale, organizational learning, and synergy are overestimated.

A third reason why an alliance may be unsuccessful is because it is *implemented poorly*. Paper benefits do not turn into reality unless a strong manager guides the process. This issue is dealt with in Section 6.

When Union Pacific and Southern Pacific merged, it was supposed to create a seamless rail service and $800m in annual savings by using UP's high-quality computer system to pull the ineffective SP up to a higher standard. However, traffic soon snarled up around SP's Englewood yard in Houston. At one point 10,000 wagons were stalled in California and Texas. Operating profits fell and the firm halved its dividend in the next year. Three years after the merger (in 1999) its share price was a third below 1997's peak of $72.

An insurer called Aetnal bought US Healthcare, partly for its computer systems, which could identify its best doctors, and partly to gain efficiencies in back offices. However, the two companies had problems combining their back offices. In another example, when Wells Fargo acquired First Interstate in 1996, thousands of the banks' clients left because of missing records, queues, and administrative errors.

A fourth reason is that, sometimes, alliances are entered into simply for the *wrong reasons*: vanity, power, and greed. Maybe the CEO wants to make their mark quickly; or the directors wanted media coverage on the financial pages; or the belief that bigger is better can prevail. Larger means more status and is associated with higher salaries, and perks such as stock options and severance pay. Fear can play a role too. Many boards are carried away by the terror that they will be bought unless they buy first – eat or be eaten. Alice in Wonderland felt that to stay in the same place, 'she would have to run faster for ever and ever, otherwise she would move backwards'.

An example of this is First, Deloitte Touche, which merged with Thomatsu, outranking Price Waterhouse. Then the latter merged with Coopers & Lybrand, outranking KPMG and Ernst & Young and reaching the number one position. Then, these two merged, recovering first place. And so on.

Finally, *cultural differences* among allied organizations can be a major problem. Culture is the personality of companies. Sometimes the fit is possible. Other times it is not. Difference of opinion is a source of diversity, and thus of wealth. The problem arises when the disagreement is about objectives – what is, and what is not, important. Then the alliance is not workable because the disagreement becomes permanent.

The alliance between the Swedish Pharmacia and the American Upjohn Inc. is a paradigmatic case. It suffered from cultural problems since its inception in 1995: management style conflicts (gradualism and consensus on the Swedish side, a decisive character focussed on results on the American); disagreement as to the incentives system (the heavy Swedish fiscal structure took the interest out of stock options); disagreement as to holiday habits (particularly the European habit of taking most of August off); rows about the 'American' practice of banning alcohol at lunch, etc. The two partners could not even agree as to the location of head office. The conflicts culminated with the resignation of the American president of the association in January 1997. After a botched attempt to make all offices report to a new headquarters in London, the company re-located to New Jersey and appointed a new boss, Fred Hassan.

One of DaimlerChrysler's cultural issues was compensation. Some American managers ended up reporting to German managers who earned half their salaries. Chrysler's boss, Robert Eaton, earned around $70m in the take-over and also earned around $6m a year. He then had to report to the more modestly rewarded Jurgen Schrempp (Daimler CEO). Schrempp tried to overcome this by suggesting a low basic salary and a high performance-based bonus. But when Chrysler tried to cut pay, the American managers threatened to depart. Egalitarian Germans dislike huge pay disparities.

Pay was not the only difference. Chrysler has a buccaneering approach, where speed and ingenuity are prized. Cars are built around common platforms, with teams of engineers, designers and marketing people working on each model. Daimler-Benz on the other hand has a traditional 'chimney' structure in which designers and marketing people mix less, and engineers are in charge. Schrempp bought Chrysler precisely to learn some of its efficient ways of working, but he had to implement it subtly: Chrysler's head of manufacturing left the new company.

One of the most successful mergers was between the pharmaceutical companies Sandoz and Ciba Geigy, which formed Novartis. The allied companies were based in the same Swiss town, run by managers who had done national service together and had a great closeness of approach. No cultural differences there.

So, alliances have *costs and risks* (lack of synergy; too costly in terms of premiums, royalties, or sales and profit sharing; implementation failures; wrong reasons; and cultural differences), but they can also have potential gains (faster results, better efficiency, entry into more attractive segments, improved strategy, and higher synergy).

There are two lessons to take away. First, costs must be weighed against benefits as shown in Figure 6.3. Second, a rule based on experience should be used. Since enthusiasm over the prospect of an alliance may lead managers to overestimate benefits and underestimate the costs, a planned alliance should go ahead only if the potential benefits outweigh the potential cost by at least 25 percent[4] in terms of expected impact on the bottom line. Otherwise it becomes too risky and the planned margin may be eaten up by expectations

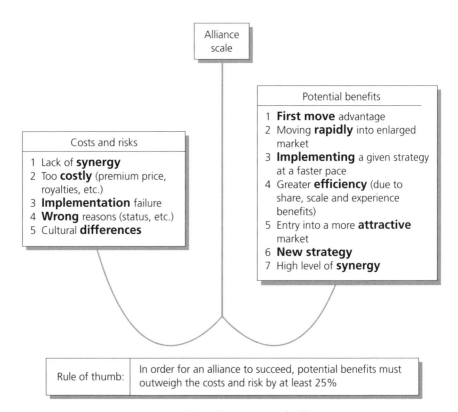

Figure 6.3 ◆ Advantages and disadvantages of alliances

that did not materialise and unforeseen costs. In such cases, it's better to go it alone – or look for a different partner.

The burden of proof lies with an alliance; the benefit of the doubt stays with continuing alone. One way to play this is to opt for contention management. Have someone on the board play devil's advocate and prepare a document listing all the known costs and risks of the alliance. This board member should not come from top management because top management is likely to press the benefits of allying. We return to this issue in Section 6.5.

Having concluded an alliance is worth pursuing, what form should the alliance take?

6.4 Choosing the type of alliance

There are two issues in choosing an alliance:

1 What is our objective? To strengthen our defense in a given segment? To enlarge another geographically? Or to enter into a new market segment? In other words, what is the *key driver*? Strategy determines alliances – alliances do not determine strategy.

2 Which alliance best suits our strengths? What have we *to offer* and what do we lack?

If we wish to buy time and speed up entry into a given geographical area, some types of alliances can immediately be ruled out: technical protocols; exchange of board members; vendor–buyer agreements. Consortiums are inadequate if this is to be a long-term step, but a merger is too great a step, because of the impact on the rest of the organization.

Five types of alliance remain: private brand and commercial agreements, joint ventures, franchises, and acquisitions. To select one, we need to look at what we have to offer. What are our strengths?

Figure 6.4 shows that if we have it all (strengths in manufacturing, image, marketing, knowledge of the local market, and financing) then the best and simplest way to buy time is through an acquisition. But if we lack financial resources, the right option is franchising. If we also lack local know-how, a joint venture will help. If we need marketing, a commercial agreement would do. If our strengths are in manufacturing, a private label deal should be established.

If a company wishes to speed up its entry into a given geographical area — And it has **strengths** in:	Manufacturing	Brand/image	Marketing	Local market specifics	Financial resources
Then it should **opt for**:					
1 Acquisition	Yes	Yes	Yes	Yes	Yes
2 Franchise	Yes	Yes	Yes	Yes (little relevance)	No
3 Joint venture	Yes	Yes	Yes	No	No
4 Commercial agreement	Yes	Yes	No	No	
5 Private label agreement	Yes			No	

Notes:
1 Dual marketing is a case in-between private label agreements and commercial agreements, where neither allied organization has strong brand image, or both organizations have equal brand image.
2 Joint ventures can be established for other reasons, such as not being legally possible to acquire a company. This is an exceptional case.

Figure 6.4 ◆ What do we have to offer?

We now have the information to decide when and how to establish an alliance.

6.5 Choosing when and how to ally

There are ten essential steps to follow when choosing when and how to ally. The first six (Sections 6.5.1–6.5.6) discuss whether allying is the right thing to do. Assuming it is, Sections 6.5.7 and 6.5.8 show how it should be addressed. The last two (Sections 6.5.9 and 6.5.10) discuss implementation. These steps are summarized in Figure 6.5.

If		How	Implementation
Content	**Process**		
1 Define the strategy clearly 2 Define the objectives to be gained from the alliance: time? efficiency? or 2.1 effectiveness? 2.2 (See Figure 2.3 6.2) Allow for one level only of 3 strategic move upgrading (Figure 6.6) Benefits must outweigh costs 4 by at least 25% (Figure 6.3)	5 Set up devil's advocate to report to the board 6 Compute benefits and costs in terms of increased economic profit (not return on assets, equity or earnings per share)	7 Eliminate any alliances (in Figure 6.1) that do not implement the defined objectives 8 Among the remaining types, eliminate those that do not address our weaknesses	9 Make a detailed and timed plan of all operational changes to be carried out to create the potential benefits and keep costs under control 10 Give the implementation of the plan to an organiza-tional heavy-weight

Figure 6.5 ◆ Ten steps to sound alliances

6.5.1 Define the strategy clearly

There are no good alliances unless they help implement a sound strategy. A good alliance is one that helps pursue a well-selected path.

Thus, the form of alliance depends upon what strategy has been selected: expand geographically, or hold the ground? Perform a counter-attack, or a blockage? In short, strategy determines alliances.

This strategy must be clearly defined. Which segments, which industries, and which geographical areas are we targeting? By defining which areas we are *not* targeting, we recognize our focus – the importance of the 'no' again. This makes the 'if' and 'how' easier to identify.

6.5.2 How does an alliance help in implementing the strategy?

What are the objectives and how can they help the defined strategy? As Figure 6.2 indicated, there are six key objectives:

1 First move advantage.

2 Capacity to occupy an enlarged market.

3 Speed up resource allocation process.

4 Greater efficiency (due to share, scale and experience benefits).

5 Entry into a more attractive and/or synergistic market segment.

6 Perform more difficult strategic moves (e.g. a frontal attack instead of a flanking movement).

Therefore, the fundamental questions are:

◆ What do we want to achieve?

◆ How does that fit with our present strategy?

6.5.3 Use alliances to upgrade strategic move by one level only

One of the advantages of alliances is allowing a different strategic move. A firm can only do so much with a given strategic move. But alliances are multipliers of strengths, so more criteria can be met.

Caution advises not to take this too far – don't expect an alliance to be able to change a guerrilla movement into a frontal attack. The jump is too great.

As a rule, alliances should seek no more than one level of higher complexity (see (b) in Figure 6.6).

There is a similar ranking for defense. The easiest strategy is withdrawal. If we are considering this, then an alliance might allow us to hold the ground. And so on. The rule again is one step at a time. Figure 6.6(c) illustrates this.

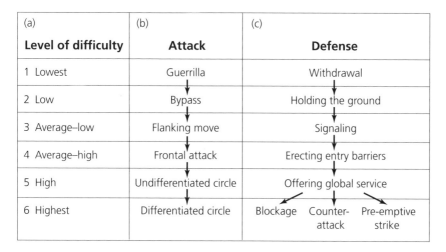

(a) Level of difficulty	(b) Attack	(c) Defense
1 Lowest	Guerrilla	Withdrawal
2 Low	Bypass	Holding the ground
3 Average–low	Flanking move	Signaling
4 Average–high	Frontal attack	Erecting entry barriers
5 High	Undifferentiated circle	Offering global service
6 Highest	Differentiated circle	Blockage Counter- Pre-emptive attack strike

Figure 6.6 ◆ Alliances allow one step change in strategy

Blockage, counter-attack, and pre-emptive strike are the most difficult defensive movements.[5]

Therefore, it is better to use the alliance for small improvements rather than aiming too high too fast.

6.5.4 Potential benefits must outweigh potential costs and risks by at least 25 percent

Figure 6.3 illustrates this.

6.5.5 Use contention management by setting up a devil's advocate function in the board

Someone outside top management should scrutinize the planned alliance and indicate all the reasons why it might go wrong. The board can then make a balanced decision. The rule requires board independence and a definition of board approval.

6.5.6 Benefit and cost computations must be done in terms of their impact on profit, deducted from the cost of capital

Other measures such as EPS (earning per share), ROI (return on equity or assets), or simply sales and asset size are subject to manipulation and/or do not guarantee maximum shareholder value.[6]

This is the last step in deciding whether or not to go ahead with an alliance. If the answer is yes, the next task will be to select the *best type* of alliance.

6.5.7 Eliminate alliance types that do not fit the defined objectives

Some types of alliance (licensing, commercial agreement, consortiums) will be adequate to implement the defined objectives. Eliminate the ones that do not.

6.5.8 Eliminate the types that do not address our weaknesses

What are the weaknesses we want minimized by the alliance? A short list will define the best alliance types.

We now turn to implementation.

6.5.9 Make a plan and timetable for all required organizational changes to harvest benefits and keep costs under control

The longer the list, the more concessions a company will be forced to make – thus the less attractive the alliance. The list usually includes:

- ◆ Lay offs (how many, from which departments, how to make selections, cost of severance packages).
- ◆ List of all assets to be sold.
- ◆ Departments to be centralized.
- ◆ Movement of managers from one division to another to transfer knowledge.
- ◆ Creation of cross-divisional consultancy boards to provide divisions with feedback on their plans.

◆ Establish new internal rules and procedures.

◆ Re-define the organization chart, position holders, and definition of functions.

◆ Re-evaluate the required internal processes: control, information, incentive systems.

6.5.10 Select an organizational heavyweight to implement the step plan

This person must have cross-functional authority, meet a specified timetable, be able to indicate costs transparently, and report to the whole board as well as top management.

6.6 Conclusion

We have identified 13 alliance types and then described the roles they can play.

◆ There are six roles of alliances: first move advantage; occupying an enlarged market at a faster pace; speeding up resource deployment; increasing efficiency (due to larger share, scale and experience benefits); entering a different segment; implementing a different strategic move.

◆ Alliances are *time savers* and *strengths multipliers*.

◆ Alliances involve *costs* and *risks*. Lack of synergy, increased direct costs (stock premium, royalties, etc.), implementation failures, cultural differences, and wrong reasons are the main ones.

◆ To keep costs under control and realize the benefits that alliances can bring, we need two things: a detailed plan of objectives and strong management.

◆ There are ten steps to follow in order to decide whether to make an alliance, which alliance to choose, and how to implement the alliance – see Figure 6.5.

◆ Strategy determines alliance.

◆ Because alliances are risky, caution is required.

However, alliances can be very useful in implementing the six attack and eight defense moves, especially in new geographical areas and where there are new customers.

7

Case study: lessons from the Japanese car industry in a global age

"The sound strategist offers battle only after victory has been guaranteed."

Sun Tzu

"The Japanese came from nowhere after World War II . . . to achieve global leadership in industries thought to be dominated by western impregnable giants: cars, motorcycles, watches, cameras, optical instruments, steel, shipbuilding, pianos, radios, TVs, audio equipment, calculators, copying machines."

Philip Kotler

7.1 Introduction

Globalization,[1] trade liberalization, new economic blocs, and deregulation have opened new markets to companies worldwide. Internationalization, however, is the most difficult form of attack. It adds three new disadvantages to the usual six – new geographical areas, new customers, and the fact that the attacker is usually smaller, relative to the new area, than it has been at home.

As we have already seen, however, small firms need strategy more than larger ones, since they do not have the resources to extricate themselves from strategic mistakes.

Japanese car companies are an excellent example of the principles of attack and defense when internationalizing. Japan's car manufacturers came from nowhere to dominate the world's markets. Toyota is now the largest car company in the world in terms of market capitalization. Honda is fifth. American and German companies now trail behind Toyota – DaimlerChrysler is second, General Motors third, Ford fourth, Volkswagen sixth, and BMW seventh.

Japanese cars have also made significant inroads into the US market. Until the 1970s it was dominated by American companies – GM, Ford, Chrysler, and American Motors. Chrysler acquired American Motors in 1987 and was itself acquired by Daimler-Benz in 1998. By 2002 the picture in the USA was as follows:

1 General Motors

2 Ford

3 DaimlerChrysler

4 Toyota

5 Honda

In August 2003, Toyota overtook DaimlerChrysler for the first time, with 12.8 percent of market share compared to Chrysler's 11.8 percent.[2] GM, Ford, and DaimlerChrysler together had a share of 57.9 percent, the lowest ever.[3]

How did Toyota achieve such success? By following, explicitly or intuitively, the principles in this book.[4]

7.2 How Japan used strategy to succeed

Ten years after World War II, the Japanese auto industry was practically non-existent. Their total output was 20,000 cars. In 1958, exports to the USA numbered precisely 288. The word Japanese was a synonym for 'cheap, low quality, unreliable products'.

7.2.1 Phase I: defense of the internal market through entry barriers

The first step for Japanese car manufacturers was to concentrate on the home market. They lacked image, had no overseas experience, and were aware that the products lacked quality, even by the standards of the low price range.

Toyota, Honda, and Mazda used the internal market to learn how to improve quality (experience benefits) and achieve lower costs (through scale economies and the learning curve). Mazda made its first passenger car in 1960. Only in 1970 did it began exporting to the USA. Toyota decisively entered the US market in 1965, more than a decade after it began producing vehicles.

Improving quality whilst reducing prices requires two things. First, heavy investments in training, mass production techniques, value analysis, (achieving savings in the parts and components less valued by customers), and its reverse: product development (investing in the characteristics customers value the highest).

The second requirement was time for the learning process to run its course. A captive market, closed to foreign competition, helped this. Japan constructed entry barriers to foreign manufacturers – import tax, foreign direct investment control, quotas, and exchange rate barriers and captive clients.

Japanese companies adopted five of the entry barriers described in Chapter 4: (1) lobby for legal and technical barriers; (2) build market and share at the fastest possible pace; (3) concentrate on success factors (value analysis and product development); and (4) move quickly along the experience curve. The government of the time provided the fifth barrier – maximizing synergy. Not among various segments, but among industries; its 'Industrial Rationalization' plan supported a close alignment of the auto, machine tools, and steel industries.

Figure 7.1 illustrates how Japanese car companies used fixed barriers to defend the internal market.[5]

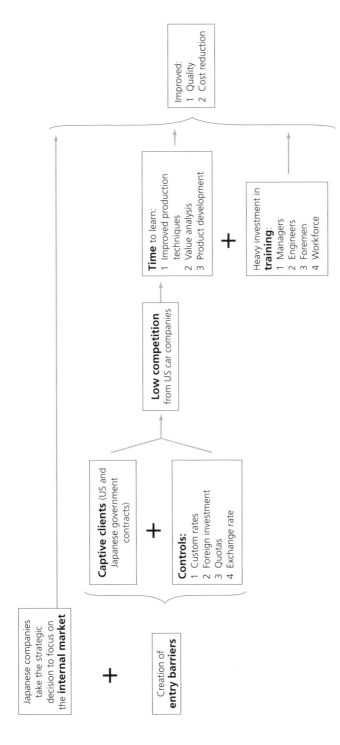

Figure 7.1 ◆ Phase I (Defense): Japanese firms erect **entry barriers** and concentrate on the **internal market** to learn how to improve quality and reduce costs

From a production rate of 20,000 in 1955, Japan was producing over
500,000 cars by the 1960s. It was now time to look overseas.

7.2.2 Phase II: attack through bypass and geographical concentration

In the early 1960s Europe was still suffering economically from the after-
effects of World War II. There was no indication of the booming economy
that Japan would later become. The only obvious export market was the USA
– that was where the money was.

But the US market posed several problems. General Motors, Ford, and
Chrysler dominated it.[6] Imported cars counted for less than 2 percent of
the market. To American customers, US manufacture meant quality, European
production passed for dubious, and Japanese meant cheap, inferior goods.

How did Toyota decide deal with the three obstacles of ignorance of the
US market, powerful competitors, and customer reluctance? It started by
researching the US market extensively. It analyzed the competition. And
finally it created an organization that would offer value to American consumers.

The market research used three information sources: foreign statistics, a
customer and distributor survey, and industry consultants.[7] This led to two
major outputs: first, a segmentation matrix similar to Figure 7.2; and second,
market research evaluated each segment's attractiveness in terms of present
sales volume and estimated margin, and also in terms of forecasted growth.

The segmentation matrix presented alternative market entries. Any segment was theoretically possible. To concentrate its resources, Toyota did not
want to enter the US market in more than one segment, which ruled out differentiated or undifferentiated circles. Of the remaining possibilities, guerrilla
attacks were the easiest. Then bypass, then flanking, with frontal attacks as the
most difficult.

Which segments could be entered by guerrilla or bypass? Competitor
analysis of General Motors, Ford, and Chrysler could show which segments
they offered models in, and which they did not. That knowledge would
enable Japanese firms to enter the US market whilst avoiding direct confrontation with the market leaders.

Such segments are marked in different shades in Figure 7.2.[8] Within
guerrillas and bypasses there were several options: motorcycles; subcompacts;
low and high-priced sports cars;[9] luxury cars over $150,000,[10] and all-terrain
vehicles priced above $40,000.

Cars \ Clients	Social classes						Organizations
	A	B	C_1	C_2	D	E	Public/ private
Motorcycles	••••••••••••••••••••••••••••••••••••••						••••••••••••••
Subcompacts	\\\\\\\\\\\\\\\\\\\\\\\\						\\\\\\\\\\
Compacts	////////////////////////						//////////
Super-compacts	▓▓▓						▓▓▓
Station wagons	▓▓▓						▓▓▓
Vans (and light trucks)	▓▓▓						▓▓▓
Luxury — Below $70k	/////						////////
Luxury — $70–150k	///						////////
Luxury — Above $150k	\\						////////
Sports — Below $40k	\\\\\						
Sports — $40–70k	//////						
Sports — Above $70k	\\\						
Minibuses							////////
Buses							////////
Cargo							////////
Special purpose vehicles — All terrain (four-wheel drive) — Below $40k	//////////						////////
Special purpose vehicles — All terrain (four-wheel drive) — Above $40k	\\\\\\\\\\						\\\\\\\
Special purpose vehicles — Armored vehicles, ambulances, etc.							////////

▬▬▬ Frontal attacks: most important segments (at least 15% of turnover) for the three dominant companies (General Motors, Ford and Chrysler)

/// Flanking: least important segments: less than 5% of total company turnover

\\\ Bypasses: segments where the dominant firm is not present, but which are close to the dominant firm's segments

•••• Guerrillas: segments where the dominant company is not present and which are dissimilar to segments they are present in

☐ Empty or scarcely populated segments: e.g. no luxury or super-compact cars are sold to lower social classes C2, D and E. No organizations other than car rental companies buy sports cars, and there are few sales here

Figure 7.2 ◆ **Segmentation matrix of the US transport vehicle industry (in US dollars at 2003 prices)**

How to choose? Two criteria were used. First, how strong was the specialized competition in each?[11] Second, how attractive were the segments (in terms of sales, value, margin, and growth)? The more attractive a segment and the weaker the competition the better.

In the early 1960s, the motorcycle segments were dominated by Harley Davidson, an all-American symbol. Popularized worldwide by the movie *Easy Rider*, Harley Davidson represented a way of life.

In the upper end of the all-terrain segment, competition was very strong: from British Leyland and especially from Jeep. At both ends of the sports car segment, competition was also strong. At the high end there were the European models: Porsche, Maserati, Lamborghini, Ferrari, and some Lotus models. At the low end there were Alfa Romeo's cheaper models, the Triumph, the Sunbeam, and Fiat's X19. The medium range was the big three's domain, with GM's Chevrolet Corvette, Ford's Mustang, and Chrysler's Daytona. The more expensive Alfa Romeo and Lotus models also belonged here.

In the luxury car segment, limousines above $150,000 for institutions were also dominated by the big three. For individuals there were European brands such as Rolls Royce and Bentley.

Besides competition strengths, the *image* of Japan as a manufacturer of cheap products made it impossible for Toyota to introduce sports or luxury models, or expensive all-terrain vehicles. Therefore, the best remaining option was subcompacts. Subcompacts also offered another advantage: they were the surest way to keep industry leaders at bay.

Since the subcompact profit margin was lower than that of the larger models (compacts and super-compacts) offered by industry leaders, GM and its rivals had little incentive to block Toyota's entry by offering their own subcompact. If they had done so, they might have ended up cannibalizing their own profits and sales in other segments. Toyota satisfied one of the major criteria recommended in Section 3.3 when performing a bypass: entry should be into a lower unit margin segment than those of the industry leaders.

As a result, despite seeing Toyota's sales jump at a yearly growth rate of 45 percent, the three market leaders hesitated, then lacked the will, and finally abandoned the idea of following suit.

Happily for Toyota, the US market leaders did not dominate in subcompacts. The segment leader was German – the Volkswagen Beetle. Competitor analysis revealed that the Volkswagen Beetle had several weaknesses in consumers' eyes:

◆ Little leg room.

◆ Lack of arm rests.

◆ Uncomfortable ride.

◆ High fuel consumption.

So competition was weaker in subcompacts. But what about *attractiveness*? Market research on consumers and distributors indicated that Amercians' traditional love of cars as status symbols was waning. Some customers were looking more at cars as a simple means of transportation. They wanted less expensive cars (in terms of purchase price, fuel consumption, and maintenance) and wanted them to be more practical – to cope with traffic congestion and be easier to park.

In other words, there was a demand for subcompacts. As this demand was not satisfied by the Beetle, there was opportunity for Toyota, so in 1965 it launched the Corona, priced at $2000 – but not across the USA. It launched in a concentrated geographical area that was as near as possible to Japan, and also was attractive – California.[12]

Geographical concentration facilitated low price and quality: it was easier to select, train and control the dealers. Proximity to Japan allowed for low transportation costs, which also kept costs (and price) under control. Finally, California was an attractive market: it had a large, wealthy, young population and there was a large Japanese migrant community.

Toyota had achieved a *double concentration*: one model (subcompact); and one geographical area 'the West Coast'. Toyota's bypass attack hurt the dominant players' sales because it stole some of the customers of the Falcon, Valiant, and Corvair. Figure 7.3 (a), (b) and (c) illustrates all this.

7.1.3 Phase III: holding the ground while erecting entry barriers to indirect competitors and performing a frontal attack on the market leader, Volkswagen

Having achieved inroads into the US market, Toyota focussed on consolidating its position. Strategically that meant three things. First, holding the ground. Second, erecting entry barriers to prevent blockage by indirect competition and by GM, Ford, and Chrysler. Finally, performing a frontal attack on the main subcompact competitor, the VW Beetle.

As Chapter 4 showed, holding the ground is facilitated by four factors: larger size, synergy, experience, and resource quality. Toyota used the latter two.

The key to experience benefits was price and promotion. The Corona was initially priced at $2000. Similar models cost between $1000 and $4000 dollars (the Vega). The Corona price was decreased by 20 percent over a

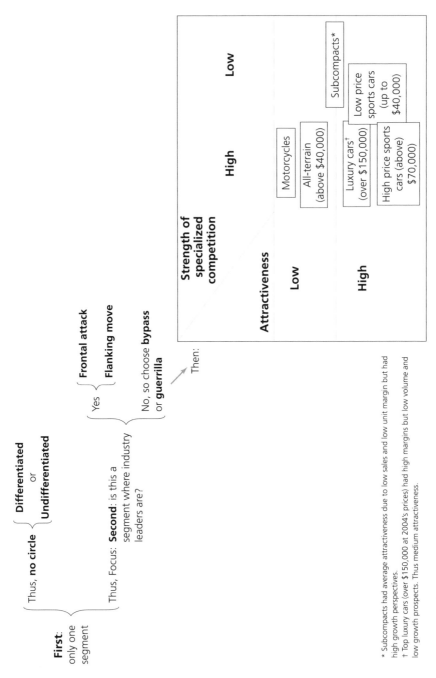

First:
only one
segment

$\left.\begin{array}{c} \textbf{Differentiated} \\ \text{or} \\ \textbf{Undifferentiated} \end{array}\right\}$ Thus, **no circle**

Thus, Focus: **Second**: is this a
segment where industry
leaders are?

Yes $\left\{\begin{array}{l} \textbf{Frontal attack} \\ \textbf{Flanking move} \end{array}\right.$

No, so choose **bypass**
or **guerrilla**

Then:

**Strength of
specialized
competition**

		High	Low
Attractiveness	**Low**	Motorcycles / All-terrain (above $40,000)	Subcompacts*
	High	Luxury cars† (over $150,000) / High price sports cars (above) $70,000	Low price sports cars (up to $40,000)

* Subcompacts had average attractiveness due to low sales and low unit margin but had
high growth perspectives.
† Top luxury cars (over $150,000 at 2004's prices) had high margins but low volume and
low growth prospects. Thus medium attractiveness.

Figure 7.3(a) ◆ Phase II: Toyota's attack via bypass and geographical concentration

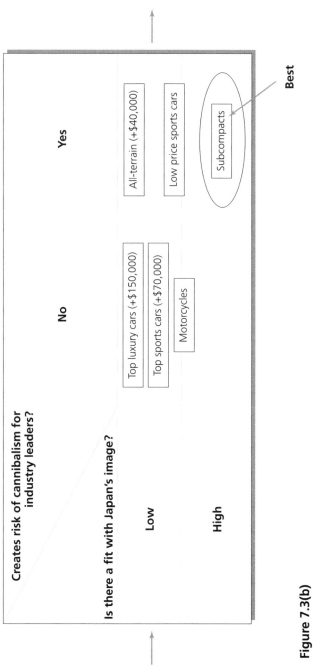

Figure 7.3(b)

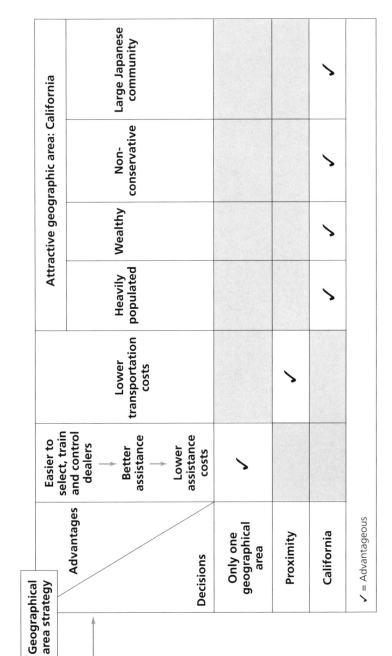

Figure 7.3(c)

ten-year period. The lower price increased sales, which led to higher production, which created lower unit costs, and thus in turn increased margin.

Then there was promotion. Toyota promoted intensively: three times more per unit of cars sold than American Motors.[13] Again, more promotion led to higher sales, which led to higher production, which created lower unit costs, and thus higher margin.

The end result was a virtuous cycle with the final result of higher share[14] and profits (see Figure 7.4).

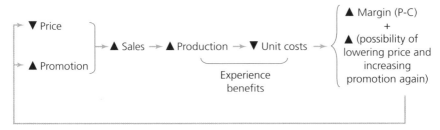

Figure 7.4 ◆ Toyota's price and promotion policies at work

Lower unit costs meant better productivity. In 1958, Toyota's productivity was 1.5 cars per worker per year. In 1965, productivity was up to 23 and in 1969 up to 39. GM's ratio in 1959 was 8.9 and 11.4 in 1969.

Sales impact on lower unit costs was magnified by four production factors. First, a high quality engineering staff led by Tyuichi Nakagawa, who had designed the engine for fighter planes in World War II.

Second, quality control circles were a constant source of creative ideas for both process and product improvements.

Third, a zero defect program was developed with the objective of identifying root causes of less than satisfactory productions. As a consequence, end-of-line defects fell to under 1 percent.

Finally, 'kanban' – just in time supply – kept inventory levels at a minimum. This was achieved by locating suppliers in the same industrial parks as the factories.

So holding the ground was facilitated by moving rapidly along the experience curve. There was also a second facilitator: having strengths in key success factors. The subcompact segment has four such factors: fuel consumption; maneuvrability; price; and design.

Corona's fuel consumption was less than the Beetle's and also lower than its indirect competitors (Pinto, Vega, Falcon, Valiant, Corvair). It decreased a further 30 percent in the next ten years.

Maneuvrability was high due to Corona's small size and the fact that it was the first imported car to have automatic transmission.

Price was another variable where Toyota had advantage. As we have already seen, the introductory price was lower than its nearer competitors and decreased 20 percent over the next decade until the Corolla was introduced at a 20 percent lower tag price. This gradual reduction was enabled by experience effects and other savings. The unit cost per car of marine damage in 1966 was $18 per car; by 1967 this had diminished to $6; and a few years later it was $3.

Maintenance costs were lowered thanks to good servicing and spare parts capacity. Toyota had 384 dealers and $2m invested in parts before introducing the Corona in 1965. Initially, dealers were picked selectively: only dealers with import experience were chosen. By 1967 almost 50 percent of these dealers were exclusively Toyota. Toyota invested heavily in training, incentives, show rooms, sales promotion and a sophisticated computerized system for spare parts. The cost of TV and media advertisements was shared on a 50–50 basis between Toyota and the dealers.

The fourth success factor was design. The Corona was an attractive car with tinted glass. The interior had the high specification required by American customers, including soft upholstery.

The major obstacle to holding the ground came from the fact that it required a frontal attack on the segment leader: the VW Beetle. However, Toyota was able to execute such an attack successfully since it followed the three rules outlined in Section 3.5: it entered only one segment (the subcompact) and fought directly with only one competitor (VW) – thus there was focus. Third, not only did Toyota identify the competitor's weaknesses (by using market research and dealer surveys) but acted on the information received: more leg room, arm rests, a smoother drive, and lower fuel consumption. It also offered twice as much horsepower and over time implemented small but continuous improvements in emissions and car safety.

Experience effects and success factor strengths also constituted barriers to the entry of indirect competition. If GM, Ford, and Chrysler had decided to enter, the barriers might have been insufficient, due to the size of these players. But they opted not to do so, for fear of cannibalizing their own sales in the more profitable segments.

Figure 7.5 summarizes this discussion. Toyota held its ground, performed a successful frontal attack, and, combined with the absence of any blockage by indirect competition, became number one on the West Coast in subcompacts.

Action		Strategy	Holding the ground and creating fixed entry barriers to indirect competition		Performing a frontal attack on Volkswagen Beetle	
			Experience and size benefits	Strength = success factors	Focus	Advantages in weaknesses
Price		Low introductory price	✓			
		Decreasing 20% over time	✓	✓		
		Excellent dealers and maintenance (decreasing its cost)	✓	✓		
		Heavy promotion	✓	✓		
Savings	Production	Marine damage (from $18 to $3 per car)	✓			
		Quality control circle	✓			
		Zero defect program	✓			
		'Kanban' (just in time production)	✓			
		High quality engineering team	✓			
		Fuel consumption — Low at start		✓		
		Fuel consumption — 30% decrease over 10 years		✓		
		Design (tinted glass, soft upholstery)		✓		
		Maneuvrability (Size, automatic transmission)		✓		
		Only one — Segment: subcompact			✓	
		Only one — Competitor (VW Beetle)			✓	
		More leg room				✓
		Arm support				✓
		Smoother driving				✓
		Lower fuel consumption				✓

Figure 7.5 ◆ Phase III: Toyota consolidates its position

7.1.4 Phase IV: geographical expansion

Toyota had now consolidated its inroad into the USA. But California, Oregon, and Washington were only a small fraction of the USA. The obvious next move was to expand geographically. But always in the subcompact segment – and with the Corona.

Four guidelines were followed. First, Toyota expanded eastwards in a solid movement. Nevada and Arizona were first, and Utah, Texas, and Louisiana followed.

Second, it moved progressively, i.e. not attacking all states at the same time. Only when a dealer network had been solidly established, when sales were up and the market position strong, was another geographical move considered. This careful use of time allowed for focus and concentration of resources.

Third, it avoided more conservative states, those with a lower urban population and fewer large cities. These states were less receptive to small cars. Toyota also avoided demographically poorer states: Mississippi and Alabama in the south; West Virginia, Colorado, Nebraska, and Oklahoma in the midwest.

Fourth, it created 'pools' of states where Toyota's presence would be mutually reinforcing: Nevada, Utah, and Arizona in the west; Connecticut, Massachusetts, and New York in New England; and Texas and Louisiana in the south.

State pooling generated strong dealerships because they could be chosen, trained, and controlled effectively. It also allowed for a lower spare parts inventory, which improved servicing and the impact of promotion.

Toyota's geographic expansion is summarized in Figure 7.6.

This expansion was accompanied by two other factors. The fixed barrier strategy (low price and heavy promotion) was repeated in exactly the way it had been implemented on the West Coast, and a new element was added: mobile barriers, of which the Corolla was the first example.

7.1.5 Phase V: adding mobile barriers to fixed barriers

Toyota began its repetition of the Californian defensive strategy by investing heavily in dealers and assistance. There were more than 1000 dealers by 1970, from a total of 384 in 1965. Toyota gave master franchises to influential and knowledgeable distributors in large areas, then allowed them to use their market expertise to recruit other smaller dealers within their territory. Complaints dropped from 4.5 percent in 1969 to 1.3 percent in 1973.

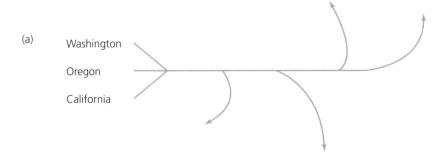

(a)

Washington

Oregon

California

(b)

Benefits / Guidelines	From west towards east	Progressively (not all states at once)	Avoiding some states	Pooling states together
Maintenance in the added states benefited from West Coast presence	✓			
Concentration of resources and focus of effort		✓		
Less eager to buy small cars — More conservative			✓	
Less eager to buy small cars — Less urban population*			✓	
Less eager to buy small cars — Lower concentration in cities*			✓	
Less wealthy			✓	
Better assistance				✓
Increased promotion				✓

* Not the same thing. A state could have low urban population (e.g. only 25% in cities) but all of it confined to a single highly congested metropolis.

Figure 7.6 ◆ Phase IV: geographical expansion

Quality of dealerships was improved by marketing programs such as Project Image, the goal of which was to help distributors improve their salesmanship through deeper understanding of customers and better personal communications. Dealers were also given high margins per unit of cars: $181, equivalent to that of much larger cars such as the Chevrolet.

Heavy promotion was a repeated characteristic. In 1971 Toyota's share of imported cars ads on TV was 39 percent. Nissan's was 19 percent. Volkswagen averaged only 16 percent.

Experience benefits in quality and price were achieved through factory automation: Toyota adopted specialized robots and multi-spot welding machines in various parts of the assembly line.

Dealership excellence. Heavy promotion. Continuous improvements in manufacturing processes. But none of these variables were new. They merely illustrate how Toyota replicated its initial defensive strategy across the USA: move aggressively, occupy the ground, and create fixed barriers.

As the fixed barriers were repeated, the mobile ones were too. The first new model was the Corolla, which had improved stability; larger vehicle tread; enlarged body; lower fuel consumption; lower emissions; improved safety; and it was faster. It cost $1800, some $200 less than the Corona's introductory price. These innovations emerged from market research and dealer surveys. Figure 7.7 illustrates the mobile barriers.

The Corolla went through an evolutionary process: its 1.1 liter engine was upgraded to 1.2 liters, and then to 1.6 liters with the Tercel Corolla model. In 1979 the fourth generation appeared and in 1984 the fifth generation was introduced with front-wheel drive and a coupé version.

Between 1965 and 1972 the Corona sold one million cars. By the mid 1970s Toyota was selling 290,000 cars annually and by 1975 it was the leading importer of passenger vehicles.

Inevitably, US companies complained. Henry Ford II estimated that for every 1 percent increase in car imports, 20,000 jobs were lost in the USA. And the American government reacted: in August 1971 President Nixon imposed a 10 percent tariff on all imports.

Despite this, in the last five years of the 1970s, Toyota's car sales grew at an astonishing 14 percent yearly rate. By 1980 sales were near 600,000 units per year, accounting for 25 percent of all imported cars. Toyota now dominated the subcompact segment in the USA. So, with its market position solidified, it was time to move on. Disposable resources could be applied somewhere else. But where?

Type of barrier / Action		Reinforcement of **fixed** barriers	New **mobile** barrier (Corolla)		
			Volkswagen weaknesses	Subcompact segment success factors	Others
Dealerships	Quantity	✓ (384 ⟶ +1000)			
	Quality	✓ (Image program, etc.)			
Promotion		✓ (39% share of imported car TV ads)			
Manufacturing		✓ Automation program			
Miscellaneous (price reductions, etc.)		etc.		etc.	
Improved stability			✓		
Large tread			✓		
Enlarged body			✓		
Lower fuel consumption			✓	✓	
Lower price			✓	✓	
Improved safety					✓
Lower emissions					✓
Faster					✓

Figure 7.7 ◆ Phase V: Toyota adds mobile barriers

7.1.6 Phase VI: jumping from one segment to another – bypassing again

Toyota asked the important question, 'Where are the industry leaders not present?' once more. The answer was motorcycles, both in the very low and very expensive sports segment, luxury cars over $150,000, and all-terrain vehicles priced above $40,000.

It then asked the second question: 'In which of those segments is specialized competition weaker?' Harley Davidson was strong in motorbikes. Porsche, Ferrari, Lamborghini, and Maserati were hard to dislodge in the highest-priced sports cars. Rolls Royce, Bentley, and Jaguar brought European glamour and prestige to luxury cars. British Leyland and the American Motors Jeep dominated the high end of all-terrain vehicles.

The only suitable area was lower-priced (below $40,000) sports cars. There was no dominant player here, but several competing head on. They were mostly non-US companies: Alfa Romeo, Triumph, and Fiat.

The third question was: 'Has this segment higher unit margin than the others?' The answer was 'yes'. Sports cars, even at the lower end, give higher margins per car than cheaper vehicles.

But what counted for Toyota's purposes was the crossover between low- and medium-priced sports cars – they are to some extent substitutes. Therefore, if the big three were to block Toyota's entry into the low-priced sports segment by launching a competing brand, they would be cannibalizing sales of their own intermediate-priced sports models (in the $40–70,000 range): GM's Chevrolet Corvette; Ford's Mustang; and Chrysler's Dodge Daytona. So there was no incentive for the major players to block Toyota.

The fourth question, 'Is the segment attractive?' was answered by market research and dealer surveys. There was increasing demand for such cars. Potential customers shared five characteristics with customers of higher-priced sports cars: they were relatively young, highly active, charismatic, impulsive, and generally male.

There was also a sixth, important, characteristic: the potential customers were willing to buy a sports car only if it was cheaper than the rivals' offerings. Demand for low-priced sports cars came from men in their 30s and 40s who either didn't have the finances or didn't want the guilt of buying a 'toy'. Frequently, the low-priced sports car was a second car.

Finally, the low end of the sports cars segment was more compatible with Toyota's image as a manufacturer of subcompacts and Japan as a producer of cheaper products than the high-end sports cars or luxury cars.

So Toyota had found a segment where the industry leaders were not present, where specialized competition was weaker, where blockage by industry leaders was unlikely since it would mean cannibalism, and where the segment was attractive: 'good margins and high growth potential'.

The resulting car, the Celica ST, was launched in the state where the demographic profile was right, California, and expanded rapidly to the rest of the US market, profiting from the already established dealer network.

The rest of the story was a repetition of what Toyota had done with subcompacts. Low price and heavy promotion moved the company rapidly along the experience curve. Strengths in the success factors constituted entry barriers. Competing models were studied to find their weaknesses and to discover how to perform successful frontal attacks on Alfa Romeo, Triumph, and Fiat. Mobile barriers (successive innovations) were introduced, i.e. the Celica Supra in 1979. And so on.

7.1.7 Phase VII: the circle

Toyota continued to add new models, always searching for poorly served segments where the competition was weak, and only later moving towards other parts of the market.

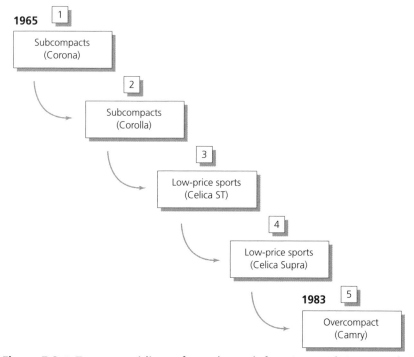

Figure 7.8 ◆ Toyota avoiding a frontal attack for 18 years (1965–1983)

It took Toyota 18 years from its 1965 entry to finally make a frontal attack on the big three US companies (Figure 7.8), which it did by entering the overcompact segment with the Camry in 1983. Eventually, Toyota moved into the luxury segment with the six- and eight-cylinder Lexus for $40,000 and $80,000 respectively (at 2004 prices). Both were part of a circling strategy by Toyota.

7.1.8 Other Japanese companies follow suit

Honda, Mazda, Suzuki, Yamaha, and Kawasaki followed in Toyota's foot-steps. The first Honda car was the S360, a two-seater, low-price sports car. This was followed by the two-cylinder N360 and N600, subcompacts roughly the size of a Mini and intended to replace larger motorcycles. Next came the Civic (sized between a subcompact and a compact, with three doors, front-wheel drive, 1.2-liter engine). Larger Civic models with four and five doors, four-wheel drive, and more powerful engines followed. These were clearly compacts. So it can be said that the Civic brand covered the market from the top of the subcompact segment through all compact niches.

Honda then moved upmarket with the overcompact Accord and the high-priced sports (NSX), the Stream (station wagon), Acura Legend (luxury), and then added the HRV (low-price all terrain), and CRV (high-price all terrain).

So Honda eventually surrounded the big three US companies. However, it entered the USA through bypasses (a low-priced sports car and a subcompact), and stuck more closely to the lower rather than the upper end of the market (see Figure 7.9).

Mazda's first car was the subcompact two-door 360 Coupé. New models created mobile barriers: the Carol 600 and the GLC. These were followed by low-priced sports cars: the Cosmo 110S and the RX7. Then a compact was introduced (the 626 Capella). And so on.

So consolidating fixed barriers with mobile barriers was a key strategy.

To summarize, Japanese firms entered the US market at the low end by adding new segments that avoided direct confrontation with the leaders, GM, Ford, and Chrysler. By the 1980s they dominated the US car industry avoiding competing head on with the leaders in the early stages.

The Japanese companies went on to repeat this behavior elsewhere – Finland and Switzerland in the early 1960s; Holland, Belgium, and Luxemburg in the late 1960s; Norway and Sweden in the early 1970s; the UK in the mid

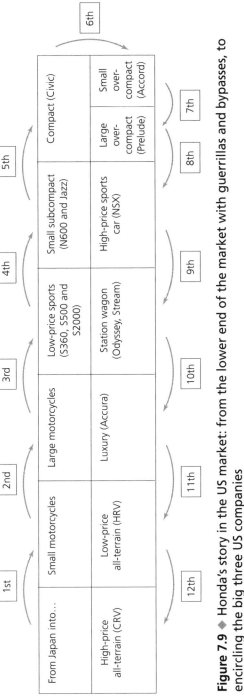

Figure 7.9 ◆ Honda's story in the US market: from the lower end of the market with guerrillas and bypasses, to encircling the big three US companies

1970s; France and Germany in the late 1970s; and Italy last in the early 1980s. Each time they chose the area with the weakest national car industry. That is, they used flanking movements to choose their targets for two decades.

Honda, Suzuki, Yamaha, and Kawasaki adopted the same technique with motorbikes. With the US market dominated by Harley Davidson, the Japanese companies started with 50 cc motorcycles, well away from Harley Davidson's 1000 cc and up models. They gained share and established their credibility. Only then did they launch a 125 cc model, then a 175 cc bike, later a 250 cc cycle, etc. All bypass strategies.

By 1966, Honda, Yamaha, Suzuki, and Kawasaki controlled nearly 90 percent of the lightweight US motorcycle market. In the UK, where the former leaders were Triumph, BSA, and Norton, the Japanese market share was 74 percent. In Germany they achieved 70 percent against BMW.

By 1975, Honda was offering 25 different models, of which 12 were off- and on-the-road combinations; 7 on-the-road; and 6 off-the-road. Kawasaki had 22 models, Suzuki 24, and Yamaha 29.

Honda waited 20 years until they dominated the smaller niches before performing a frontal attack on Harley Davidson with the 1000 cc Goldwing.[15] By 1981 Japan was producing 7,410,000 units, representing a global market share of 65 percent. It exported four million motorcycles, mostly to the USA, Europe, and the Far East.

Harley Davidson did nothing, believing that their 'motorcycles are sports vehicles, not transportation vehicles . . . It is generally for leisure time use. The lightweight motorcycle is only supplemental. Back around World War I a number of companies came out with lightweight bikes. We came out with one ourselves. We came out with another one in 1947 and it just did not go anywhere. We have seen what happens to these small sizes . . .'[16]

Eventually, Harley Davidson filed for bankruptcy and applied for – and was granted – a quota on Japanese motorcycle imports from the government of the time.

This is the first reason why sometimes the leaders do not react: *errors of evaluation*. This is sometimes because of arrogance ('we know better than the consumers what their wishes are'). At other times, the leader's passivity is induced by fear of cannibalizing its own sales.

Today, Japan is world leader in motorcycles. Their strategy and success against Harley Davidson has been repeated in other countries against other brands. The end lesson is the same. Use segments and niches to avoid initial

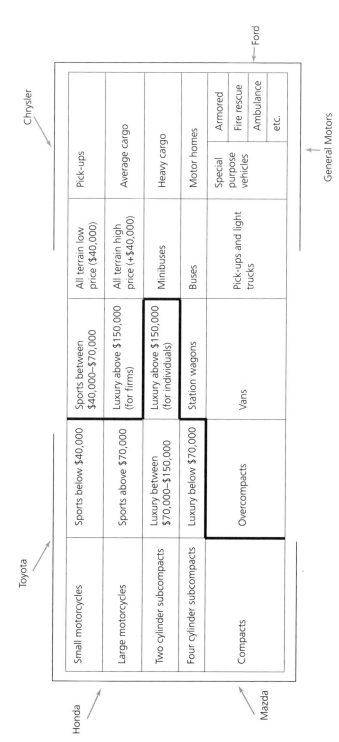

Figure 7.10 ◆ How Japanese companies divided the US automobile market without confronting the dominant players

head-on competition with the industry leaders. Jump from one segment to another. Defend your segments through erecting fixed and mobile barriers to indirect competition and frontal attacks on direct ones. Grow profit. Improve your market share. And before the leader knows it, you will have divided the market with it without confronting the leader directly. As Sun Tzu put it: 'Battles should be given only after victory has been guaranteed'.[17] Figure 7.10 demonstrates this.

7.3 Lessons to be learnt

Toyota and the other Japanese car-makers illustrate some of the rules we have been working towards in this book and apply them to internationalization.

First, defense should precede offence. Before internationalizing, products and services should be tested in home markets, where there is greater knowledge of geography, customer psychology and suppliers and distributors. Even without some degree of formal or informal barriers, careful segmentation will avoid (or at least minimize) competition.

This means that internal markets are the ideal playground for testing and adapting products. Mazda focussed on the home market for eight years from 1962 before exporting to the USA in 1970. Toyota also concentrated on the home market. Lag time between offering the product internally and abroad is especially important in the first steps in internationalization. As experience gathers, that becomes less important.

A second important guideline is the T-rule (see Figure 7.11). In home markets, large firms are frequently in many segments. One segment is not usually enough to sustain a large company, and domestic competition is often not strong enough to force the company to specialize, so it moves into other segments.

This is not the case when internationalizing. One segment will now be large enough because there are so many different countries and geographical areas. Besides, competitors are likely to be larger and stronger. So, internationalization means changing from geographic specialization and segment expansion, into geographic diversification and segment specialization.

The general rule is – the larger the market, the more specialized a firm should become in order to prosper. Globalization thus becomes an opportunity to narrow product lines.

1 **First defense** (the home market), then **attack** (abroad).

2 When attacking, **change** from geographic concentration and product extension into geographic diversification and product concentration.

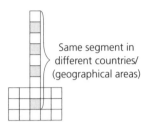

Same segment in different countries/ (geographical areas)

3 **Segment characteristics**:
  3.1 One segment only (focus).
  3.2 Success factors = company strengths.
  3.3 Look at easy options first – guerrilla before bypass, etc.
  3.4 Lower unit margin than leader's segments.
  3.5 Synergistic.
  3.6 Attractive (sales, volume and growth).
  3.7 Culturally compatible (with home country's image).
  3.8 Weaker direct competition.

4 **Geographical area characteristics**:
  4.1 **One at a time**, after market share consolidation.
  4.2 Where there is **a** segment with characteristics of (3) above.
  4.3 Where the **same** selected segment exists.
  4.4 Proximity:
    4.4.1 Distance; and
    4.4.2 Culture.
  4.5 High potential (population, GDP per capita).
  4.6 Adequate for own model/product (climate, lifestyle, etc.).
  4.7 Cluster (for joint support).

5 **Later, there is a choice between**:
  5.1 Moving among segments within the same geographical area; or
  5.2 Adding geographical areas to the same segment(s).

6 **Within 5.1 there is the choice between**:
  6.1 A snake strategy (avoid major competition); and a
  6.2 Chain strategy (enhance synergy).

7 **Alliances**:
  7.1 Yes, or go alone?
  7.2 If yes, which of the 13 possible types?

Figure 7.11 ◆ **Lessons from Japanese internationalization**

Moving from broadly focussed domestically into narrowly focussed globally requires a careful selection of the segment(s). Ideally there should only be one, and at most a few; and they should be the same across geographical areas, to benefit from scale economies and experience benefits. It generates focus. The selected segment should be attacked by the simplest method – guerrilla is the method of choice, and differentiated circle is the last option.

The Japanese gained acceptance in electronics and computers as suppliers of original equipment and private label manufacturers.[18] They developed by marketing differentiated products through selected dealers. In the hand-held calculator market, Casio and Sharp offered various distinct features: calculators with clocks; with melodies; pocket size (a 2-mm thick card size calculator), etc.

Canon started attacking Xerox through a bypass movement: instead of large machines, it offered smaller ones; rather than selling through a direct sales force it went through distributors; in place of leasing, it sold the machines outright.

In short, the history of Japanese penetration of the US market is a poignant illustration of how segmentation and a careful chosen point of entry can change the terms of engagement. When not the leaders, the Japanese never played the game according to the rules the leader had set. Through distinctive strategies, the rules of play are changed and the leader neutralized and paralyzed – no matter how strong it is.[19]

This is helped if the chosen segment has *lower margin per unit of product sold* than the segment the competition is in (point 3.4 in Figure 7.11) In such a case, if the latter blocks our entry it will be cannibalizing its own sales. Toyota and Mazda entered the automobile industry with subcompacts. Honda, with small motorcycles. Seiko penetrated the watch industry with low-price quartz watches. Casio's first calculator was small, pocket size, and cheap. Canon started by producing small photocopying machines. Sony manufactured very small TV sets.[20]

Finally, the segment selected to internationalize should be synergistic with other segments in the home market, and attractive (at least in terms of growth potential). Toyota detected a trend towards small cars. Then the need for a lower price sports automobile. Citizen introduced the world's first solar-powered watch.

An attractive point of entry abroad can come from two sources – through identification of market segments that have been ignored or poorly served by competitors, or from opportunities created through innovation. The output can be a segment (subcompact cars) or a niche (50 cc motorcycles within the motorcycle segment). Therefore, (1) market analysis; (2) innovation; (3) segmentation, and (4) niche creation, all enable a company to choose its competitors.

Information is key. Information about consumers' needs and values leading to an industry segmentation matrix and an evaluation of each segment's attractiveness. And information about competitors, leading to a better understanding of their strategy, strengths and weaknesses.

Japanese home appliance manufacturers have a tradition of stripping down Western products (microwave ovens, automatic dishwashing and laundry machines, ovens) to their simplest parts. They then study them to evaluate their number, variety, designs, technology, cost structure, and performance. In short, information is the food for intelligence.

Then the management of geographical areas (point 4 in Figure 7.11) plays an important role in achieving success in international markets.

The chosen country must possess the segment selected for internationalization. Better a guerrilla than a by-pass; better this than a flanking movement, etc. And it helps if the geographic area is close to home – not just in mileage but also culturally. The first allows for lower transportation costs. The second for an easier understanding of how the markets work.

After being in a geographical area for some time, a company has two options. It can expand in that area by entering into other segments: product enlargement. Or it can stick to the same segment(s) and move into other geographical areas: geographical enlargement. (Here there is no contradiction with the first rule, since one is now further along the process of internationalizing.)

Product expansion and geographic concentration is logical when four factors are present: the greater the attractiveness of a specific geographic region; the stronger the synergy among segments; the more guerrillas and bypasses that can be found in the specific geographic market; and the lower the opportunity cost of expanding into other segments in terms of scale and experience benefits. When these four values are reversed, geographical expansion and segment concentration should be pursued.

In the first case (geographic concentration and product expansion) there are still two options: either to focus on synergy among segments or concentrate on competition avoidance. The first follows the motto that the strength of a chain is only the strength of its weakest link.[21] The second abides by advice from the Bible to be 'simple as a dove and cautious as a snake'. In order to decide, both the synergy and the strength of the competition must be compared.

As a general rule it is preferable in the early stages to concentrate on avoiding competition, because there are more opportunities for guerrillas, bypasses, etc., and the potential for synergy is lower. As opportunities become scarcer and the synergy potential greater (our company is now in more segments), synergy can lead the way.

As a final point, it is important to note that the Japanese do not have the monopoly on strategy wisdom. For example, German car firms such as BMW and Mercedes also entered the US market through bypasses and flanking moves, rather than frontal attacks. Sometimes the Japanese have been 'out-strategied', as when the Swiss-produced Swatch came back to fight the cheap Japanese imports – Swatch changed the rules again. There have also been political problems (the above-mentioned quotas and the fact that the yen was re-evaluated to 17 percent of its former value, which harmed exports), and labor problems (strikes forced Toyota to ship cars through Canada and Mexico). Even here, though, the Japanese mastery of strategy was shown by the fact that this idea was a contingency plan, prepared precisely in case of industrial action.

And the Japanese did make some mistakes. The first Toyota passenger cars had lights that were too dim to pass Californian standards and the engine roared like a truck.[22]

So Japanese success did not come easily, but mistakes are part of human nature and luck is part of life. No strategy will ever avoid them totally. What a sound strategy will do is minimize the blunders and offer a path for fast recovery from them.

It is better to err with the right strategy than succeed with the wrong one. With the right strategy, after the stumble one is still on the right path. With the wrong strategy, even without stumbles, one ends up in the middle of nowhere.

As Archimedes said, 'give me a place to stand and I will raise the world with my arms.'

8

Conclusion:
the eight rules to follow
to deserve success

"Austrian generals defeated in 1796 by Napoleon protested: 'It is impossible for someone to ignore so basically the most elementary principles of war'."

Ferdinand Foch, Marshal of France, Principles of War

"We all recognize a strategy when we see one."

Gary Hamel

Eight statements summarize this book's essential message.

1 Defense is stronger than attack

New market entrants face six challenges. First, the company we are attacking may have been the first company in the segment. In such cases, the brand name is associated with the product in the customer's mind: Aspirin; Coca-Cola; Kleenex; Black & Decker; Gillette; Kodak, Jeep; Band-Aid; Jello. Customer loyalty is here at its strongest.

Even if that is not the case, the defendant has five other advantages on its side:

◆ Greater market know-how.

◆ Experience benefits (learning curve).

◆ Larger market share (greater visibility and better image).

◆ Larger size in the industry (allowing for higher economies of scale).

◆ Customers' resistance to change.

It's hard to dislodge market leaders. AC Nielsen studied the 50 best-selling UK grocery brands recently and concluded that only 9 out of 50 (less than 20 percent) had been launched in the two previous decades.

Trying to grow by extending products and losing focus on core strengths is the main reason companies fail. A survey by Bain & Co. indicated that 'the major reason why many businesses fail to deliver value to customers and shareholders is that they wander too far from their core'.

When considering a strategic move, the burden of proof lies with the decision to attack. The benefit of the doubt remains with defense: using the company's resources to improve market share in the present market's industries and geographical areas.

This does not mean that a firm should never attack. Only that the odds are against it.

So when is an attack justifiable?

2 There are four criteria that must be satisfied before attacking

◆ Can the firm meet the implementation requirements? These are different for each type of attack. Most of these requirements must be met – see Chapter 3.

◆ There must be no threat of entry by a new competitor.

◆ The required resources must not be more usefully employed building share in the present markets.

◆ The new segment must be more attractive than the present ones, in terms of sales, growth, margin, and volume.

Chapter 5 offered a practical tool to help decide when to enter into new markets and when to defend one's domain.

3 There is a natural sequence for choosing a defense

Not all of the eight defense moves should be considered simultaneously. Three strategies (signaling, creating entry barriers, and global service) should be considered first.

If these will not work, the other defense strategies should be looked at in order, before considering withdrawal as a last resort. But even this can be a new beginning – saving resources to be better applied elsewhere.

This decision is about when to give up – and when to hold the ground and fight.

4 There is a natural sequence for choosing an attack

The easiest form of attack is the guerrilla. Then bypass, then a flanking move. Frontal attack is preferable to an undifferentiated circle, which is preferable to a differentiated circle.

This is because the chances of success are greater the more the strategy attacks the competitor at its weaknesses, not its strengths, does not force it to react, uses the least amount of our resources, and provides the most support for strategic business units.

5 The criteria for defense or attack must be well implemented

There are a different number of criteria for each different strategy. All are discussed in detail in the relevant chapters. A large percentage of the criteria must be met to maximize the chances of success. Success depends not only on how well a strategic move was selected, but also on how well it is implemented.

6 Strategic moves can be performed in isolation or in alliances

Alliances pursue two main objectives: buying time (increasing the pace at which resources are deployed); or multiplying strengths (augmenting skills, reducing costs).

They have 13 distinct forms, from exchange of board members and consortia (both having minimum impact), to mergers and acquisitions (maximum impact). In between, there are other forms such as private brand agreements, dual marketing, licensing, and so on.

Sound alliances must satisfy *the ten criteria listed* in Chapter 6, Figure 6.5. First the company must decide whether or not an alliance is in its interest. It must be clear how the alliance implements the defined objectives. The projected impact on profits must exceed total costs and risks by at least 25 percent, to allow for expected benefits that have not materialized, and unforeseen costs. Economic profit should be the metric – not other criteria such as earnings per share or return on assets, and should benefit from the input of a devil's advocate reporting to the board.

Alliances follow strategy. Not the other way around. And the onus of proof lies with alliances. If it is doubtful that the ten criteria can be met, an organization should go it alone.

7 Internationalization is the most difficult form of attack

There are three additional drawbacks: newness of geographical areas; newness of customers; and smaller size of entry. Since the risks are greater than in any other form of attack, it is necessary to adhere even more strictly to the rules of attack, defense, and alliance and to select among them.

The case study in Chapter 7 provides examples of successful and unsuccessful internationalization.

8 Success depends on mastering the rules of when (to perform each type of strategy); how (to implement it); and whether (to do it alone or in alliance)

Chance will always play a role. Luck is as much a part of business as of life. But the rules maximize the *chances* of success. And if we play by them we will *deserve* that success.

Notes

Chapter 1

1 There are several solid works on the so-called Zulu wars. However, two of the best books are: *Great Zulu Battles: 1838–1906* (1998) (Cassel Group: New York) and *Brave Men's Blood: The Epic of the Zulu War 1879* (1990) (Greenhill Books: London), both by Ian Knight. Much of the present text is sourced from these two books.

2 The Cape of Good Hope was named by Bartholomeu Dias, another Portuguese navigator, because in a previous journey he concluded that it was the most southern point of the African Continent and thus had to be the much desired pass into India.

3 The British demands included: to surrender some members of the royal family for trial in a British Court; to pay substantial compensation for border depredations; to change the military organization of the kingdom (i.e. abolish the 'amebutho' system under which men had to work for the king building royal homesteads, hunting, mustering for war, etc., until allowed by the king to marry); cease all internal killings; and allow all missionaries to return to Zululand.

4 They were nevertheless technologically inferior to the British since most of their firearms were obsolete. Their ammunition and power were poor and they possessed no heavy artillery. The army was divided into 'ibuthos' (groups of 4000 men) under a separate command and broken down into two wings, each under a subordinate commander. It was further sub-divided into companies of between 50 and 70 men, drawn from the same part of the country and led by a warrior selected from their ranks. Their motivation was very high. When joining the army, some warriors were chosen to kill a bull with their bare hands. The flesh was then sprinkled with magic potions and distributed among the army to bind it together and endow it with the bull's bravery and strength. Different regiments challenged each other to count the bravest deeds in the battles.

5 The total levies amounted to 40,000 men. Of these, 16,000 were scattered around the kingdom in defensive positions.

6 The types of rifles used at the time needed to be reloaded after every single shot.

Chapter 2

1 The calculator industry has several segments: desktop calculators; pocket calculators; and multifunction calculators (functioning also as clocks, personal organizers, radio receivers, etc.). Other firms such as Sharp also segmented the market to avoid a head-on fight with Texas Instruments. Sharp decided initially to focus on pocket calculators, and only expanded their scope over time.

2 Pennington, M. W., and Cohen, S. M. (1992) 'Michael E. Porter Speaks on Strategy', *Planning Review*, January, pp. 8–11, Robert J. Allio & Associates, Inc. for the North American Society for Corporate Planning.

3 *Combat Intelligence* (1973), US Army Field Manual 30–5, October, 2–13.

4 Sun Tzu, in *The Art of War*, op. cit., p. 37.

5 Ries, A. (1996) *Focus: The Future of Your Company Depends on it*. HarperCollins. See also Ries, A. and Trout, J. (1986) *Marketing Warfare*, McGraw-Hill; Ries, A. and Trout, J. (1993) *The 22 Immutable Laws of Marketing*, HarperCollins US; and Reis, A. (2000) *Positioning: The battle for your mind*, McGraw-Hill.

6 In later years IBM started to make money again, although profits were not in the same proportion to sales as before.

7 They started with the low market end (low-price PCs) and then moved next to the opposite upper end (supercomputers).

8 Ries, *Focus*, op. cit., p. 130. Also see Zook, C. and Allen, J. (2001), *Profit from the Core*. Its argument is that (1) diversification from the core can destroy the value a company promises; and (2) a firm must make sure it is reaching its full potential in its core business before expanding into adjacent surroundings.

9 IBM was to recover to an extent – see Gerstner, L. (2004) 'Who says elephants can't dance?'

10 With Iacocca as President, Chrysler Corporation transformed itself into a holding company with automobiles being just one of its businesses. It became a 'four box' corporation: Chrysler Motors, Chrysler Aerospace, Chrysler Financial, and Chrysler Technologies. Later Iacocca admitted that his biggest mistake was to diversify. 'We didn't need a holding company. That made us top-heavy. Before, if we went astray – and that happens now and then to companies – we got focussed in a hurry'.

11 So successful was Little Caesars that within a few years it was imitated by Poker's Pizza: a similar slogan, 'Buy one, take two'; very small stores (just one or at most two tables); colorful signs and merchandising to attract the attention of passers-by; and an orientation towards impulse buys. This me-too strategy is called a frontal attack, as we shall see in the next chapter. Also, the success of Domino's Pizza home delivery was soon to be imitated by Tele Pizza, which attacked the former in the home delivery segment. To change the terms of engagement to suit one's strengths and thus obtain competitive advantage is a fundamental rule in business as well as war.

12 Standard Air Service for two-day delivery was maintained but de-emphasized and so seldom mentioned.

Chapter 3

1 The industry usually distinguishes within the luxury segment between cars below US$70,000, between US$70,000 and US$150,000, and above this level.
2 All product aspects including delivery, service, non-core product characteristics (packaging, etc.).
3 It is interesting to note that the lower the social class, the more a guerrilla brand is seen as 'either/or' instead of 'also'. A customer with little money will opt for one watch, magazine or car – and uses the guerrilla instead of a more expensive major player. So the guerrilla achieves a niche. As they climb the social ladder, the customer increasingly sees guerrillas as complements to standard purchases from the major players. Sorels snow boots, Chivas Regal whisky on special occasions, etc. At the top end of the social spectrum, the customer again uses the guerrilla as 'either/or' – only the best whisky, only the Rolex will do.
4 If our company is a guerrilla regarding only one and not all three leaders, then it is performing either a bypass, a flanking, or a frontal attack. These, as we shall see in Chapter 5, are harder to achieve.
5 Any strength we can rely on: know-how, technology, delivery, etc.
6 For example, subjecting imports to tests and reducing the internal market.
7 The learning curve and scale economies are different concepts. The former is about decreases in costs since the *start* of manufacturing in the first year. That is an *experience* effect. Scale economies, however, are consequences of the production achieved *within* a given year. That is a *size* effect.
8 Some periods of politics are no different. After the French Revolution, which ended by devouring its own children (Maros, Danton, Robespierre), someone asked the Parliament member Abbé de Sieges what he had done during the Revolution. 'I survived,' he said.
9 After some time Cadillac decided to block BMW through a new model: the Cadillac Seville. But apart from this exception, BMW's series 3 and 5 models bypass all Cadillac models. Blocking is a defense strategy, which will be discussed in Chapter 4.
10 The Boston Consulting Group matrix defines a company's portfolio as one of four types of business units: cash cows (high market share and low growth), stars (high growth and high market share), question marks (high sales potential but low market share) and dogs (low in both market share and growth).
11 Ries, A. and Trout, J. (1988) *Bottom up Marketing*, McGraw-Hill.
12 Tag Heuer watches focus on strength, speed, and sport. Its marketing campaign shows athletes running against greyhounds, swimmers competing with sharks, and motorists sharing the road with aeroplanes.

13 The lower the difference among the segments, the greater the risk of cannibalism. The lower the number of models covering those segments, the less specialized they will be, and thus, again, the greater the risk of cannibalization. So cannibalism increases with the similarity among segments and decreases with the number of models (as they become more specialized):

Increased risk of cannibalism — Likelihood among segments / Number of models	Low	High
Very few*		High
Large (for each segment there is a distinct model)	Low	

Risk of Cannibalism (arrow Low → High)

$$\frac{\text{*No. models}}{\text{No. segments}} = \text{low}$$

14 To decrease the risk of cannibalism (although that risk is lower with a differentiated circle than with an undifferentiated circle, where the risk of confusion among synergistic models is greater).

15 For more on this see Ries, A. (1996) *Focus: The Future of Your Company Depends on it*, HarperCollins.

Chapter 4

1 Scale and market share advantages are related but different concepts. A firm can benefit from economies of scale in its back offices, even if it has low market share in its various industries. Or a company might benefit from the impact of market share without having to make scale economies.

2 Sun Tzu, in *The Art of War*, op. cit.

3 If this message had been addressed to the German enemy before the war, it would have been a signaling defense. As it was given during the war, its aim was strengthening resistance, not dissuading attack. It was an internal message designed to motivate and consequently create entry barriers. External messages are signaling strategies.

4 Size and experience benefits are not the same. Size benefits are economies of scale. They depend on the production volume *per year*. Experience benefits are related to the learning curve, i.e. to production *year on year*. Experience benefits depend on the cumulative volume of production since the *first unit* of

the product was manufactured, independently of the number of years of production.

5   Electronic goods firms are increasingly redefining their business from televisions or CD players to multiplex producers of televisions, video, amplifiers, radio, CD players, loudspeakers, etc.

6   The rationale for the Iraq war was to attack before it was able to use its alleged weapons of mass destruction.

7   Location can be *time* location (Shell Shops opening 24 hours a day), *geographical* location, or *distribution channels* location.

8   As discussed in Chapter 2, strategy is *where* you decide to fight (in the present segment – holding the ground – or in the segment the competitor has entered into – blockage – or in another segment we decide to enter – pre-emptive strike, etc.). Whatever the strategic decision, the tactical battle then follows: advertising the product, penetrating the distribution channels, keeping manufacturing costs down, and so on. Strategy is before the battle, tactics come afterwards.

9   The same applies to warfare. During the American Civil War, the North had 140,000 more casualties than the South. In the World War II, the allied forces lost twice as many men as the Axis Powers. This idea led Napoleon to say, 'engagement must be fought with forces proportional to the enemy'.

10 Pyrrhos, King of Epirus, defeated the Romans twice: at Heraculea (280 BC) and at Asculum (279 BC). His heavy losses caused him to declare, 'one more such victory and I am lost', thus the origin of the term 'Pyrrhic victory'.

11 All three businesses share know-how in optics and lens grinding.

12 The four businesses exploit common knowledge in semiconductors and digital displays.

13 All share a technology core of multilevel cylinder heads units self-adjusting valves.

14 They have digital switch software in common.

15 Losses can be accounting losses (if accounting sales are lower than accounting costs) or economic losses (i.e. money).

Chapter 5

1   Diversification and attack are different, though related, concepts. Diversification refers to entry into a new industry or geographical area. Attack is an entry into a new market segment (see Chapter 3).

2   Clawson, D. A. and Scott, D. (1992) *Money Talk: Corporate PACS and Political Influence* (HarperCollins: New York).

3   As analyzed in the previous chapters, the criteria is always the same: sales volume, sales growth, and sales margin.

4   The leader may ask: can we perform more than one strategic move at a time? Scott Paper, a major US supplier of paper towels and toilet tissues, was faced with strong competitive attacks from Procter & Gamble, Georgia Pacific, and

Ft. Howard Pacific. Scott simultaneously performed a withdrawal, together with counter-attacks and a flanking move. The company withdrew from sanitary napkins and tissues. At the same time, it invested heavily in toilet paper, intending to dominate the low-cost segment. It also entered the paper towel, facial tissue, certain napkins, and baby wipe segments as counter-attacks, and increased its emphasis on international areas, such as Korea and Malaysia, Mexico, Taiwan, and the Philippines, as a flanking attack.

Chapter 6

1 An example is the co-operation between Daimler-Benz and Volvo to develop engine components for aviation.

2 Alliances can be defensive or offensive. They can also be tactical, where the company's market segments remain the same; or strategic, where there is an alteration in the company's market segments.

   All attacks imply strategic change, but there is no correlation between defense and tactical alliances. Indeed, some defense alliances can be tactical: holding the ground, more credible signalling, improving entry barriers, global service. All other defensive alliances are strategic, because there is entry into new market segments.

   So, all tactical alliances are defensive (counter-attack, pre-emptive strike, blockage or withdrawal), but not all defensive alliances are tactical – four defence movements imply a change in strategy. The concept of defense alliances includes both strategic and tactical moves.

   We can have three types of alliance: 1) strategic and offensive; 2) strategic and defensive; and 3) defensive and tactical. There are however, no attack and tactical alliances.

3 Particularly joint ventures, acquisitions, and mergers, which have a greater impact on the allied organizations (see Figure 6.1).

4 This applies to both allies. The reader may ask: How can this happen? Surely for one party to gain, the other has to lose? Not at all. If this were the case, alliances would be a zero sum game and no value creation would occur. Value for both parties arises from synergy (e.g. downsizing common departments), or from each ally gaining a different benefit: one buys time, the other obtains a premium on the price of its stock.

5 It could be argued that a pre-emptive strike is more difficult to implement than a blockage or a counter-attack since it additionally requires competitor information and speed of action.

6 Any good book on EVA (Economic Value Added) explains this in detail. One recommended is Stern, J. M. and Shiely, J. S. (2001) *The EVA Challenge*, John Wiley & Sons.

Chapter 7

1 Globalization is the development of homogeneous segments across the globe, enabled by consumer exposure of similar media and more frequent contacts, as a consequence of better communications and faster transportation.

2 Toyota's worldwide sales in 2002 were 25 percent above DaimlerChrysler's.

3 The Japanese auto industry's success story is in no way diminished by Japan's recent economy problems. First, whatever problems the Japanese economy presently faces, they pale when compared to Japan's situation at the end of World War II, when. 13.1 million were unemployed. Material losses were 64.3 billion yen (at current values), equivalent to one quarter of the national wealth. Nowadays, Japan is the second world country with the highest number of companies among Fortune 500: 104 (against 185 for the USA and 141 for whole Europe).

Success is not beyond reach, regardless of the state an economy is in at the beginning or of how small a firm is initially. Second, our subject is performance abroad, so the economy at home is irrelevant. Third, economic problems at home should not hinder success abroad.

4 Japanese firms borrowed from the teachings of *The Book of Five Rings*, written in 1645 by Miyamoto Musashi, a celebrated samurai warrior. Professors Kotler, Fahey and Jatusripitak wrote a highly recommended book on the subject: *The New Competition* (op. cit.). This was used as a source for the present text and the interested reader is directed towards it.

5 Due to globalization and related phenomena, only the fifth entry barrier is easily achievable today. But it is still recommended to concentrate on the internal market first. Segmentation can play a very important role.

6 American Motors was much smaller and much less profitable than the big three. From its birth in 1954 to its sale to Chrysler in 1987, it lost money most years.

7 All of this was financed by the Japanese government. Other incentives included risk credit insurance and tax incentives: 150 percent of all export oriented investments were tax-deductible costs. However, in order to qualify for these benefits, exported products had to satisfy certain quality standards.

8 In all other segments, the industry leaders were present to a higher or lower extent. In the low-price all-terrain category (below $40,000), Ford had since 1959 offered the F250, and since the mid sixties the Bronco, later replaced with the Expedition. In the above-$40,000 segment, American Motors offered the Jeepster CJ.

Special-purpose vehicles were fragmented into several niches: school buses, ambulances, snow-removal vehicles, landscaping and dumper trucks, and armored vehicles. They were all bought by institutions that had a 'buy American first' policy. Most of these were public administration institutions.

The big three dominated these niches. In armored vehicles, GM had the 3500 and TC; Ford the Ranger, E350 and F550; and Chrysler the 3500 Dodge.

9   The industry leaders were present in the intermediate price range of sports cars.

10 GM, Ford, and Chrysler offered luxury limousines above these prices. They were mostly institutional cars. Personal cars of this price range were mostly European: Rolls Royce, Bentley.

11 As opposed to industry leaders.

12 Later on it expanded but always along the Pacific coast: Oregon and Washington.

13 In 1969 American Motors sold 270,000 cars against Toyota's 130,000. AM's promotion budget was $12m. Toyota's was $18.5m. So Toyota spent $142 on advertisement per car sold. American Motors spent $44.

14 In 1958 Toyota sold 288 cars in the USA. Twenty years later it was selling 500,000 per year.

15 To be followed by similar cc models from the other Japanese motorcycle manufacturers.

16 Quoted in Kotler *et. al.*, *The New Competition*, op. cit.

17 Sun Tzu, *The Art of War*, op. cit.

18 Over 80 percent of Toshiba's TV sales were as a private label for Sears to begin with. Radio and audio equipment was also manufactured for large retail chains' private labels.

19 Playing the game by trying to 'out-excel' the leader would have been a doomed strategy in due time.

20 Entry through the lower market end is a must when the firm is unknown and its home country has a poor image of quality. When that is not the case, firms can select other points of entry. BMW and Mercedes used Germany's reputation as a solid technology producer to enter the US car industry through the high end. The problem here is that you face a higher risk of being blocked, since the profit margin per unit of car sold is high.

21 The argument used by W. Ulbricht, former East German President, to convince other Warsaw Pact members to invade Czechoslovakia in 1967.

22 The Toyota case study also illustrates the importance of learning from mistakes. Arguably, Toyota committed three mistakes, in its early stages. The first was the Toyopet, a subcompact. As seen in this chapter the segment was well chosen, but the Toyopet did not compare well with specialized competition. The second failure was the Land Cruiser: an inexpensive all-terrain. This was a flanking movement (not a guerrilla or bypass) to Ford (which competed with the F250 and later the Bronco). Moreover, and again, specialized competition was very strong: British Leyland and the Jeep (from American Motors). Result? Failure. Third, there was the Stout, a Toyota pick-up that failed because it was nothing less than a frontal attack to *all* three industry leaders: to the Chevrolet (from GM); the F1 and F2 series (from Ford); and the Dodge (from Chrysler).

When did success knock on Toyota's door? When for the first time it chose a segment (subcompact) and a model (Corona) which satisfied all major criteria in Figure 7.11 point (3): a bypass, where direct competition was weaker; a high-potential segment, where blocking the industry leader was unlikely, and so on.

In short, not only the successes, but also the failures of Toyota stress the importance of following the criteria stated in this chapter (Figure 7.11).

Bibliography

Collins, J. C. and Porros, J. I. (2002) *Built to Last: Successful Habits of Visionary Companies*, HarperBusiness.

De Wit, B. and Meyer, R. (1998) *Strategy: Process, Content, Context*, Thomson Learning.

Fiévet, G. (1992) *De la Stratégie Militaire à la Stratégie d'Entreprise*, InterEditions.

Greene, R. and Elffers, J. (1998) *The 48 Laws of Power*, Viking.

Hamel, G. (2002) *Leading the Revolution: How to Thrive in Turbulent Times by Making Innovation a Way of Life*, Plume.

Hamel G. and Prahalad, C. K. (1994) *Competing for the Future*, Harvard Business School Press.

James, B. (1986) *Business Wargames*, Abacus.

Kotler, P. (2002) *Marketing Management*, 11th edn, Prentice-Hall.

Kotler, P., Fahey, L. and Jatusripitak, S. (1985) *The New Competition*, Prentice-Hall.

Kotler, P. and Singh, R. (1981) Marketing warfare in the 1980s, *Journal of Business Strategy*, Winter 30–41.

Linneman R. E. and Stanton Jr., J. L. (1991) *Making Niche Marketing Work*, McGraw-Hill.

McDonald, M. and Dunbar, I. (1995) *Market Segmentation*, Macmillan.

Moore, K. and Lewis, D. (2000) *Foundations of Corporate Empire*, Prentice-Hall.

Porter, M. E. (1998) *Competitive Strategy: Techniques for Analyzing Industries and Competitors*, Free Press.

Ries, A. (1996) *Focus: The Future of Your Company Depends on it*, HarperCollins.

Ries, A. and Trout, J. (1986) *Marketing Warfare*, McGraw-Hill.

Ries, A. and Trout, J. (1993) *The 22 Immutable Laws of Marketing*, HarperCollins US.

Robert, M. (1999) *The Power of Strategic Thinking: Lock in Markets, Lock out Competitors*, McGraw-Hill.

Robert, M. (1993) *Strategy Pure & Simple: How Winning CEOs Outthink Their Competition*, McGraw-Hill.

Rogers, D. (1988) *Les Stratégies Militaires Appliquées aux Affaires*, First.

Sammon, W. L., Kurland, M. A. and Spitalnic, R. (1984) *Business Competitor Intelligence*, Wiley.

Sawyer, R. D. (1996) *Unorthodox Strategies for the Everyday Warrior*, Westview.

Slywotzky, A. J. (2002) *The Art of Profitability*, Warner Books.

Slywotzky, A. J., Morrison, D. J. and Andelman, B. (1998) *The Profit Zone*, Wiley.

Trout, J. (2000) *Differentiate or Die: Survival in Our Era of Killer Competition*, Wiley.

Trout, J. and. Rivkin, S. (1996) *The New Positioning*, McGraw-Hill.

Vasconcellos e Sá, J. (1998) *The Warlords*, Kogan Page.

Vasconcellos e Sá, J. (2002) *The Neglected Firm*, Palgrave.

Index